THERE SHE GLOWS

FEATURING
LINDSAY NASH

Disclaimer:
In parts throughout this book, the authors may have tried to recreate events, locales and conversations from their memories of them. In order to maintain their anonymity in some instances we have changed the names of individuals and places, we may have changed some identifying characteristics and details such as physical properties, occupations and places of residence.

Although the co-authors and publisher have made every effort to ensure that the information in this book was correct at press time, the co-authors and publisher do not assume and hereby disclaim any liability to any party for any loss, damage, or disruption caused by errors or omissions, whether such errors or omissions result from negligence, accident, or any other cause.

CONTENTS

INTRODUCTION
MAYBE YOU KNOW HER?

She's the woman who never gave up on her dreams...
She is brave, she is courageous, she is kind,
She is the dreamer, the believer... the glow getter.
She listens to the daily whispers that tell her she is meant for more...
much more...
And she is ready to leave her footprints in the sand.
To live a life of uncompromised dreams
A life that is true to her
A life that reflects her version of extraordinary.
It's time to...
Let go of the past,
Trust in the future,
Embrace change,
Be brave enough to come out of your cocoon,
Unfurl your wings,
Dare to get off the ground,
Ride the breeze,

Savour the flowers,
Put on your brightest colours,
Let your beauty show.
You were born to do wonderful things, so believe in yourself and dare to dream again.
The power is within you to be the change in the world you were always meant to be.
We hope you find Comfort.
We hope you find Love.
We hope you find Belief.
We hope you find the strength to chase your dreams.
And more importantly we hope you find the LIGHT that is you so that you can GLOW.
There... She... Glows.

OUR MESSAGE

"It's OK to be the Glow stick: sometimes we have to break before we can shine."

Welcome to the very first volume of the *'There She Glows'* book collaboration series launching as part of Glow Society's™ global sisterhood supporting women just like you. I am so incredibly grateful that you have found us, or maybe we have found you. I don't believe it's any coincidence that you are here. There will be certain lessons, blessings, words of wisdom and encouragement that you have been waiting to hear, or perhaps a reassuring message that allows you to feel less alone in your world.

Maybe you still have so many dreams left unfulfilled, so many memories you still want to create and maybe you know (deep down) you are capable of achieving, and living so much more than the life you are currently living.

Maybe you are being called to step into your potential with a new vision for your life and business but you're not sure how to make the change or where to begin.

Maybe, like I used to be, you're paralysed by the gap that bridges you from where you are to where you want to be, full of doubt, worry and limiting beliefs.

Maybe you're lacking the confidence and clarity to follow through on your own dreams, overwhelmed by the noise and what everyone else is doing.

Maybe you're tired of trying to find your place in the world and create success, whatever that means to you, but you can't break free.

I hear you; this was me too. I spent years rewriting the same goals with no idea how to break free, start over or recreate this inspiring vision I had for my life. For years I was so disillusioned with a bank balance and lack of fulfilment that did not reflect my worth, or how I wanted to feel. However, I write this to you today as a four-times Best Selling Author, six figure Business Coach, the founder of my own company (Glow Society™) and living a life that reflects my dreams and highest values. Everything, for a long time, I never believed I was capable of creating or having.

I am standing in the shoes of the women I wish I had met over ten years ago when I made the bold decision that I would no longer accept a life of 'normality', and instead follow my dreams in creating true happiness, fulfilment, success, abundance, wealth, and freedom. A life that has since allowed me to breathe again. Those who know me and have read my journey from past publications will know that this was not always my reality. In fact, I endured over ten years of heartache, disappointments, sloppy investments, a million personal development books, the heaviness of low self-worth and many moments of 'rock bottom' to get where I am today. I felt like a 'nobody' for so long and very much lived in the shadows of others, never feeling enough on my own. I used to drown in comparing myself to everyone else in the online world, exhausted with trying to make the entrepreneurial dream work for me. I had a bank account that was paralysing and looking back now I actually don't know how I survived the many months of inconsistent (sometimes zero!) income.

Whilst I don't want to make this introduction about me and my story (*you're welcome to find out more about my journey from previous books I have authored*), I do wish to shine a light on the truth of my success because I know in doing so you will feel less alone. Because there was a BIG journey for me in finding my own light, authentic voice, and the confidence to feel valuable enough to the world. This gap is really my big vision and purpose behind Glow Society™ because I very nearly gave up on my dreams (many times), and I am forever grateful that I didn't. Just remember, everything you have been through to date hasn't all been for nothing. Miracles always take a bit longer than settling does so be patient and I promise the dots will eventually join. And suddenly you will glow a little bit differently. You will no longer feel like your place in the world is lost and you will be standing tall, as you.

> *"Like a wildflower, she spent her days allowing herself to grow. Not many knew of her struggle. But eventually all knew of her light."*
>
> — *NIKKI ROWE.*

Glow Society supports women from across the world through taking them on a journey of self-discovery, soulful awakening, and transformational alignment (in life and business) so that they can live with more fulfilment, purpose, and meaning, doing what they love. We want to bring you home to the magic that is already YOU, the REAL YOU because we know this will transform and shape the way you are experiencing life and all you deserve it to be, as well as your current results. Glow Society encapsulates everything I needed and wish I had had access to during my journey of growth and success.

I look back now and can see that every lesson was a blessing, every challenge was an opportunity and every dark day has equipped me to now shine that little bit brighter for the wonderful community of ladies within the Glow Society. Our biggest mission is to ensure women like you always have the support, love, guidance, community, tools, and friendship to never give up on your dreams, no matter how bleak your reality might look today. We encourage you to let go of any shame from your past failures, the goals you didn't reach, the relationships that you allowed to rob you of any self-worth, the bad decisions that cost you time and money. We encourage you to instead walk forward and create your new 'once upon a time'. Your time is now, and everything has been leading you to this part of the journey. This I promise you. The world needs you and Glow Society is here to be your guiding light to wherever your path may lead. I desire nothing more than to see you shine and glow as the true women that you are.

> *"Your purpose is what you say it is. Your mission is the mission you give yourself. Your life will be what you create it to be."*

— THE SECRET.

I would love to extend a special invitation from me to you with love.

Glow Society has provided an extraordinary sisterhood consisting of beautiful, empowering, supportive women from around the world. Our online community provides people with the opportunity to come together to connect, get encouragement, share best practices, support one another, inspire each other, and so much more and I would be honoured to extend that invitation for you to join us too.

Maybe you are searching to find your path to financial freedom.

Perhaps you are looking for the capacity to feel happy and fulfilled every day.

Or maybe you just want to create the time to do what you love with who you love every day.

Maybe you need the belief to follow through on your dreams.

The clarity to bring your vision into fruition.

The trust in yourself to step out of the shadows and into your light.

We have got you, and we welcome you with open arms. Our community is driven by love, encouragement, friendship, inspiration, and we hope to support you in fulfilling your highest purpose and potential, whilst creating aligned wealth and freedom.

We value:

FAMILY

'Where life begins and love never ends.'

~

FREEDOM

'The opportunity to be and live like you never thought you could.'

FINANCIAL SECURITY

'Having your heart and mind free from the "what-if's.'

AUTHENTICITY

'Unbecoming everything that was never really you to be who you were always meant to be.'

LOVING RELATIONSHIPS

'The best and most beautiful things in the world cannot be seen or even heard, but must be felt, to yourself, to others, for others.'

UNCOMPROMISED DREAMS

'Let your dreams be bigger than your fears and actions be louder than your words.'

∾

MAKING MEMORIES

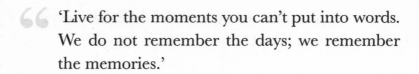 'Live for the moments you can't put into words. We do not remember the days; we remember the memories.'

A LIFE FULL OF CHOICES

'Is a life well lived.'

IMPACTING THE WORLD

'In a gentle way you can shake the world.'

SUCCESS

'You deserve to make a difference and be recognised for that.'

FAITH.

'The confidence in what we hope for and assurance about what we don't see.'

We really are the home where:
Dreams are seized,
Purpose and Potential is pursued,
Love and alignment are attained,
Wealth and freedom are created.

We walk together to leave our old stories behind us and instead follow everything that lights us up.
In doing so we light up the world.

WE GLOW

We welcome you to join our Global Sisterhood here:

www.glow-society.com

https://www.facebook.com/groups/glowsociety

So here we are, launching the very first volume of the *There She Glows* collaboration book series. Partnered with eleven incredible women from around the world, I want to take this opportunity to thank them all for contributing their incredibly inspiring stories of which I share in absolute awe. I salute every single one of them for having the courage to share their truth, their messages, and their lessons to inspire the rest of the world. I have complete gratitude and love for them all and am honoured to have provided Glow Society, and the There She Glows Collaboration series as a platform for making it possible. So, if you will come with us on this journey, we will take your hand and support you in getting to the highest and most inspired vision for yourself, life, and business.

> *'To everyone else it looks like a single leap. But in reality it was hundreds of little baby steps.'*

Here is my final message of love and inspiration that I want to leave you with before I hand you over to the amazing co-authors of this book.

The bamboo tree takes five years to break through the ground. It required five years of nurturing, attention, watering and love. If you miss a day, it dies. But once it breaks through the ground, within five weeks it grows ninety feet tall. So don't worry if your journey to date has required a little bit (or a lot!), of nurturing which has created a lack of confidence in your ability to ever get there. I know how you feel... I lived with this soul-destroying feeling for a long time. Finding your calling and achieving your purpose is never a straight road. Sometimes we just need to stop, breathe, pivot, and come home before we can break free.

> 'The canvas is blank, it's never too late to create your masterpiece.'

LUCY CRANE - VISIONARY BEHIND GLOW SOCIETY™

Entrepreneur, Speaker, Business Success Coach, Founder of Glow Society™, and 4x Best Selling Author.

With over eleven years of experience in business and entrepreneurship, Lucy has worked with thousands of individuals and business owners in the online and offline space and proudly supports women all over the world with her One to One Coaching, Online Programmes and Global Community - Glow Society™.

Lucy is incredibly passionate about making a global impact on people's lives and truly believes that everyone has the potential to create and live their own version of extraordinary. With freedom being at the forefront of her values and the way she chooses to live, she is a huge advocate for High Ticket Transformation and Automation and she shares this with her clients so that they can escape the social media hamster wheel and instead create a business they love which allows them the capacity to be truly present and free with who and what matters most in their world.

You can find out more about working with Lucy on a One to One basis, or her Online Programmes by visiting:

www.lucy-crane.com.

Lucy has been recognised for her many achievements and the positive impact she has continued to make in people's lives through media publications including London Business Magazine, Thrive Global, Eloquently Her, as well as being featured on "That's TV Oxfordshire" and will continue to share Glow Society™ on a global scale.

If you have a story to tell, a lesson, or a blessing to share, or specialise in an area of expertise and would like to be considered for any of Glow Society's Publications, Podcasts, and future *There She Glows* book collaborations, please email lucy@lucy-crane.com to apply.

With Love and Glow,

Lucy x

Social Media Links:

Website: www.lucy-crane.com / www.glow-society.com
Email: lucy@lucy-crane.com

f facebook.com/lucy.crane.9

⊙ instagram.com/lucycrane.glowsociety

LINDSAY NASH

'YOUR STORY IS THE KEY THAT COULD UNLOCK SOMEONE ELSE'S PRISON'

*H*ello, gorgeous souls. I am going to offer you my story in the hope that I can offer you a shining light of hope, happiness and renewed confidence if you have been or are going through a difficult period in your life; or if you are longing for change but have no idea how to get there and feel stuck.

That is how I felt most of my adult life. I now feel free, strong, secure, happy and emotionally stable.

Most of my life has been a train wreck. Childhood trauma, abusive relationships, drink and drug abuse, marriage failure, depression, anxiety, low self-esteem, self-loathing and much more. But I sit here today writing this in the hope that I can help and inspire anyone that is struggling with life to believe that no matter who you are, or what you're going through, you can change it and overcome it.

If I can then anyone can.

We are all unique and special and I truly believe that every human has superpowers inside of them, they are just often crushed by fear that leads to so much self-sabotage and unhappiness.

I have learned to understand how to cope with abandonment and rejection issues and to put a stop to it destroying the rest of my life. I have learned to love myself for me which is something I never dreamed I would ever say.

It is my mission to show you and many more women how to overcome childhood and relationship trauma, and to come out stronger and more confident than you could ever imagine possible. So buckle up and enjoy the turbulent story of how I changed my life.

'This is me now'

I am a 43-year-old single Mum absolutely smashing life and helping other Mums to do the same.

I am confident in my own skin.

I am confident in my ability to provide my children with the most amazing life full of fun, love and laughter.

I am so f*@king proud of myself and love myself for all that I am and all that I'm not.

I have many lumps and bumps and emotional scarring that I now fully understand and have learned to live with but NOT live by.

I am a work in progress and try every day to get more amazing than I was yesterday.

'Wow,' I hear you say, 'this girl is one confident and happy lady with all her sh*t together.'

Well, let me tell you some honest truth here. This girl talking to you now hasn't always been like that. I will now enlighten you as to how I went from daily car crash to the superwoman I am in the lifelong process of becoming.

'The old me, and where it all began'

I had a mixed childhood. It was blessed in some ways and turbulent and terrifying in other ways. My father drank heavily and as much as I have always been very close to him, he has always been an abusive drunk. I witnessed him abusing my Mum on many occasions when I was a child and he has disgracefully abused me verbally over the years. In many ways he gave me a good childhood, as in I had ponies and a nice house and I know he wanted us to have a great life, but unfortunately the booze always superseded the 'good times' and I don't look back on my childhood with many fond memories.

It created a lot of fear inside me and led to me suffering from very low self-esteem, fear of abandonment and fear of rejection. I trusted no one and hated who I was. Every day I wished I was somebody else living a completely different life. I was attracted to 'bad boys' and friends with similar self-worth issues and I spent my teenage years on total self-destruct.

If someone ever paid me a compliment, then I would totally dismiss it and it would make me feel so uncomfortable. I had no idea why this was and just put it down to modesty. Not realising, until my awakening, that it was due to the fact I didn't feel worthy of compliments. I never felt as good as my friends. I thought everyone was better looking than me, more intelligent than me and more important than me. I gradually forgot how to love as I was so filled with anger and depression. My self-confidence was zero.

'All I ever wanted was to become a Mummy'

I had my first baby at nineteen and I fell so in love with motherhood. I felt somehow slightly completed by my gorgeous son. What wasn't complete for me was the family unit that I so desperately craved.

I'd longed to create this family unit since my parents divorced. I wanted my children to have the perfect

Mummy and Daddy that would be there for them in every aspect of their lives.

However, unfortunately through drug addiction the father of my baby wasn't able to give me that stable family life that I so desperately wanted. Instead I was put through years of pain and turmoil trying to support him and had my heart absolutely broken. Eventually at the age of 23 and with two children together, I finally gave up on trying to save him, and realised I needed to save myself and my children.

Well, that didn't go too well and I went on to have another long term abusive relationship with a man who drank very heavily and he was extremely abusive to me when he was drunk. I put up with this for four years until, again, I could take no more and succumbed to the realisation that he was never going to change into the father figure I wanted for my children and when our baby was one year old we broke up for good.

66 'I was now completely lost but could always put on the bravest face'

So far, my life had brought me much more pain than happiness. Much more trauma than stability and at 27 and a mother of three I had no idea how the hell I was going to sort my life out.

I'd always dreamed of being successful but never ever felt I could achieve it. My life up until this point had been far too turbulent and chaotic to be able to focus on bettering myself. I had completed a few IT courses and managed to get a couple of half decent jobs, all of which I hated.

I used to come up with a new business idea every week but no courage to ever do anything about it, as there was way too much of a risk of failure, and that terrified me as I felt I had failed at everything all of my life.

'Finally I meet Mr. Right... Or so I thought'

At 27 I met my now estranged husband who was a lot more stable at the time than any of my previous partners. He was 21 and had been fortunate enough to have had a good upbringing with lovely parents. He adored me and supported me in everything.

I had finally found stability. However, I now know that I had so many issues caused by my past that it was going to take more than a quiet, level-headed boy to sort me out.

He did for a long while and we were very happy. I was stable enough to complete a full-time university degree with three small children and I graduated with a 2:1 BA Honours Degree. This was the first time in my life I actually felt like I had achieved something and I had a glimmer of hope of reaching my success goal.

My husband and I went on to have fourteen happy years. We were best friends and we completely had each other's back. We had two beautiful children together and enjoyed every moment of raising them.

Finally I had created that 'ideal family' that I had always craved.

We were so happy. We were financially secure. Owned three properties and lived a very comfortable life. The only thing missing was time to ourselves. I immersed myself in my children. I thought being a good wife and amazing mother would be enough to keep my husband happy. Unfortunately that wasn't to be and cracks started appearing.

I began to resent him for certain things that I won't mention in this book and he began to resent me for not giving him enough attention, affection and love. I was unable to give this to him because I could sense the resentment he had towards me and I felt that if I could just be the perfect mother to his children this would be enough. It wasn't.

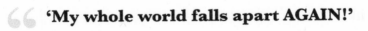 **'My whole world falls apart AGAIN!'**

My husband left the family home, and within two weeks he was with someone else. My loyalty and mothering skills proved not to be enough. He needed that excitement and fun you have when you initially meet someone. The intimacy in our marriage had died as no one attempted to keep it alive and with a house full of kids and teenagers it's quite hard to keep the 'fires burning' so he had to look for it elsewhere.

To say I was absolutely broken would be an understatement. My whole world had been ripped from underneath me. My children were all devastated as no one saw this coming.

My babies were four and seven years old and their little worlds had been torn apart. It was the most devastating time of my life. I felt so ashamed yet again that I had failed. I had failed my husband, I had failed my children and I really didn't know how I was going to get through it.

The months following the split were agonising. I could barely eat, I spent so many nights sobbing uncontrollably all night long and I was absolutely terrified. I had lost my best friend and my rock. Here I was trying to keep it all together for my five children while inside I was completely broken. The shame and guilt was massive and made me feel so ill.

Every day I put on a brave face in front of my children and kept us all so busy on little holidays and adventures. I did my crying in the dark on my own. I didn't want a pity party. I just wanted desperately to get better and it just wasn't happening.

The more my children suffered and developed signs of it affecting them mentally, the worse and more scared it made me feel until I realised after a couple of months that I had to do something about this. I had to work so hard on myself and uncover my demons and abandonment and rejection issues that were keeping me stuck in this fearful and depressive state. I had to get myself sorted and quickly for the sake of my kids but also for the sake of me too.

I had been running quite a lot since the split and this really helped me. In fact, I can honestly say it was like medicine for my anxiety and low mood. A good sprint in the mornings would really set me up for the day. I did make the mistake one day of putting on power ballads while I ran around the field outside my home. I found myself halfway around screaming uncontrollably and lying in the long grass (thankfully it was long enough not to be seen by any other dog walkers). I was unable to stand up as my legs had given way with grief, fear and anger.

I was a mess. Things had to change. I was really worried for my children as I felt completely out of control.

This next part of my story will tell you how I turned from a terrified, grief stricken, self-hating woman into a confident and happy Mum who has never felt so free and sure of the future. I have recognised my limiting beliefs and done so much work to uncover all the sh*t that was trapping the warrior inside me.

'The Rise of the Warrior'

I had delved into the self-development world in 2015 when I started network marketing. I absolutely fell in love with it and it helped me so much. I then left it alone for a while as I thought I'd learnt enough. I now know that you can never ever learn enough; you can never stop being a student of life.

So in my desperate state I literally immersed myself back into personal development. I also went to therapy which I felt also really helped me uncover my insecurities and fears and why I have them and how they DO NOT serve me. I stopped watching Netflix. I stopped wasting my time with the 'what ifs' and focused on the future.

I read book after book. I watched YouTube motivational videos. I listened to podcasts any time I could. I would always have my headphones on whenever I could listen to something positive and motivational. I completed a Life Coaching certification too which enabled me to coach myself.

I literally invested £1000s into myself as I believed the best thing in which you could invest any money you had was actually on your mental well-being, as everything in your life is a reflection of how healthy you are mentally.

From the courses and the books, one of my biggest realisations was that I couldn't continue to do what I had always done and expect my life to ever change. I needed to deep dive into my mind and my beliefs and try and undo what was keeping me stuck in a life that didn't serve me. I had to become much more open minded and put into practice all these new skills I had learned. I wanted more than anything to change my life so I was willing to be the best student and undertake anything that would assist me on my journey of healing and transformation.

I very gradually started to feel stronger and I started to develop a deep respect for myself. I learned to forgive myself for past mistakes and to stop blaming myself for everything. I know I had a part to play in my marriage breakdown, but in no way did I ever deserve to be treated the way I was after the split. It was like being stabbed in the heart and then having the knife pushed further in and twisted all of the time whilst I was trying to raise my children and keep them safe from hurt. It was so, so painful and hard to endure. I had no respect for myself at all and allowed the treatment.

'I've gradually come to realise that if you don't love yourself you can't love others and if you don't respect yourself then no one else will either'

I went from waking up daily in a state of fear and anxiety to feeling much calmer. I could sleep again at night and stopped waking in the middle of the night with the darkest thoughts and feelings.

It was the deeply ingrained fears inside me that kept me stuck and in grief mode for so long. Of course, I was devastated my marriage had failed as I took my marriage very seriously and I would have stood by my husband through anything, as one of my hardcore values is loyalty closely paired up with honesty. However, the marriage was no more, but I struggled so much to come to terms with this. I had never been single before. I had been in serious relationships since I was fourteen and I actually had no idea who the hell I was on my own. I was a wife and a mother. That was my identity.

Who the hell was Lindsay Nash?

My journey of self-discovery continued with me learning more about my core values and how becoming aligned with them in all areas of my life, such as work and relationships, would enable me to live a happier and more fulfilled life. This all started making so much sense now.

It explained why I had always felt frustrated in my relationships and always tried to change the people I was with rather than accepting they weren't right for me because of the fear that no one better would come along... God forbid me being on my own (rolling eyes).

It enabled me to really connect with my purpose and to discover who my true friends were. Friends that shared the same values and morals as me.

Nothing like a 'good ole marriage breakdown' to show you who your friends are. To be honest, I wasn't shocked by the ones who let me down and it was probably for the best. I gained some new friends, and some friendships that hadn't previously been that strong before got so much deeper and for that I was so grateful. I see it as weeding your garden. I got rid of the weeds that were preventing the flowers from growing. I now have a beautiful garden with many different flowers in it. It's a great place to be.

My wonderful tribe also included my amazing older children who just stepped up and showed their remarkable strength, resilience, courage and diplomacy in what was such a painful situation for them too.

I was so proud of them, and it displayed to me that although I gave myself a hard time about the mistakes I had made when they were small, I had clearly done a good job of raising three well grounded, kind and intelligent human beings.

I allowed myself to be proud of me for this. In fact, I started allowing myself to develop pride in my past and present achievements. I actually started complimenting myself and saying well done to me when I achieved a breakthrough in my mindset and understanding of myself and my emotions.

I went from self-loathing and no confidence to learning how to love myself and put myself first. Sometimes even before my children which had always been unheard of.

This would never be to the detriment of their mental health, such as neglecting them when they needed me or dating, as they weren't ready for me to do that; the fact their Daddy got with someone else and had another child so soon tore their world apart so the last thing they wanted was their Mummy off jollying around with someone else. This was fine with me. I was on a mission of self-discovery and knew that once I had healed properly I would be in a much better position to enter into a new relationship. One that would be healthier and happier than I had previously ever experienced. I was happy to wait.

They needed me full time. They needed an intense amount of love and made to feel secure after what had happened. That was what I was prepared to give them. Even if it took the rest of my life. I would give them anything they needed love-wise to help prevent them developing the same issues that I developed as a child and so many other children do from broken homes.

I was at this time studying personal development for around six hours a day! I had discovered something called 'transformational psychology' combined with brain science and it was very quickly changing my life. My self-esteem was flying through the roof compared to the hurt and embarrassed woman of months before. I was learning how to control my thoughts that led to my emotions and then to my actions. I was beginning to see life through a completely different lens than the one I had been viewing it through all of my life.

'I learned that change had to be done from the inside out to be sustainable'

So up until this point in my life I had always dreamed of achieving great things but never had the confidence to do anything about it. I didn't think I was worthy of money or abundance in any form. I didn't think I was worthy of anything other than mistreatment, really, when you consider what I allowed to happen to me all of my life.

I dreamed of financial freedom in my own right and to be completely independent and able to give my children a life full of wonderful experiences. I wanted to travel the world with them and enable them to discover different cultures and ways of living. I dreamed of starting a children's charity and opening it up with all my children standing next to me and taking their part in it too.

I was one of those people who would start off with all the intentions of changing and sticking to a plan to change my life, only to give up after a few weeks and return to old habits.

I would start diets and quit, gyms and quit, money making schemes and quit, jobs and quit. In my head I was a quitter. So guess what? I lived up to my story and quitted everything I started to make my life better. I never felt good enough to succeed or worthy of success. My stories in my head, created by a lifetime of limiting beliefs, always got the better of me and brought me back to my comfort zone. Success is scary, Lindsay, I heard my monkey mind say. It's not for people like you.

We will always return to familiarity and our old ways of being. We always go back to our identities.

'You can never outperform your identity'

I had now learned that if I wanted to achieve all of this then I needed to change my identity. I needed to change all of the labels I had given myself through the bull sh*t stories that I had created in my head as a child and throughout my younger years.

This didn't mean changing who I am at the core but it meant identifying who I was subconsciously. Who I conformed to being on a daily basis; and changing that person.

I had learned that you can only make sustainable changes in your life if you change your core beliefs about who you are: 'your identity'.

So, armed with all my months of heavy study, my coaching qualification and my love for transformational psychology, I began to unpick my subconscious. I was changing my belief systems and the new and improved Lindsay Nash was being created and she was really quite amazing. She had always been there but my old self who hated me had basically sat on her and not allowed her out. Occasionally she may have peeked out and made some noise but my old self jumped straight back on top of her and shut her up as she made the old me very uncomfortable suggesting she do brave things such as 'sort her f*'king life out!'.

This new confidence was growing inside of me. Confidence I had never felt before. Not the sort of confidence that you need to stand up and speak in front of a load of strangers but an inner confidence. An overwhelming feeling inside that everything was going to be ok and life was going to be bloody amazing. The anxiety was gone. The fear was gone. The constant nagging in my head that my life wasn't where it should be was gone! I felt freer than I'd ever felt before. I had found spirituality.

I knew exactly who I was, exactly what I wanted, and I knew how I wanted to live my life in line with my core values. I had come to realise that up until now I had no idea who I truly was. All I knew was that I was a scared little girl with no direction, a belly full of worry, a head full of stress and a heart full of pain.

I felt almost like I'd been reborn. I didn't have to walk around faking confidence and happiness anymore. I'd never been a person to show my true feelings… 1. Because I didn't really understand them… and 2. Because I hate pity. So I never really told anyone how I felt about my life. In fact, this

Chapter and my website is the first time I have actually expressed how much pain I have endured throughout my life. I've always pretended I'm fine. However, it is clear from my actions and life choices I was certainly never 'fine'.

I no longer cared what people thought about me and my fear of rejection was no longer controlling me. I now knew I had the courage and knowledge to start my own business helping other women just like me gain their power back.

'Mum Warriors was born'

Once I knew that I wanted to start an online business so I could reach as many women as possible, I literally dived right into creating Mum Warriors. It felt in total alignment with my soul. I have been through so many difficult struggles and traumas that many women face over their lives and I have mastered skills to totally transform my identity and therefore transform my life into one of peace and harmony.

I live in a complete state of faith in my intuition and in the universe. I know what I have to do. I am a woman on a mission to help as many women as I can develop strategies in their lives to increase their happiness, confidence and belief in themselves, so that they can get out of their own way and start living a life that no longer fills them with fear and anxiety. I help them to find out who they are and implement huge changes in their lives so that they can be the best role models to their children.

'You are the lens to the world for your children.'

So what you do, they will do.

When someone said that to me, I felt so sad for my kids.

I felt like I'd let them down.

I now know that I'm showing them how to get what you want in life. How to break through fear and the barriers we create in our minds, and to live our lives on our terms without the need for the approval of others. Without fear of judgement. Without fear of failure. I show them how to live for now and to enjoy the journey without focusing on outcomes.

Once you learn to live how I have learned to, then the sky's the limit. The possibilities are endless as there is no wall. There are no mental blocks. There are no regrets, as I see everything as a lesson and a giving. I am grateful for everything, including the tough times as they're there to serve me as much as the good times. You gain so much strength and courage from adversity if you just allow the lesson to flow through you.

When you learn to stop resisting change, start accepting what is, and live happily with what you have, then your life starts filling with good people and opportunities.

Without me even consciously knowing it, I have filtered out the unhealthy and negative people in my life and my life is now full of gorgeous souls that illuminate me and are such positive influences on me and my children.

'Become so positive that negative people can't bear to be around you'

The key to creating true fulfilment and less stress is you have to own everything you do and understand that life is due to your choices.

Although it wasn't my fault that my childhood at times was turbulent and scary - it was my parents - it is totally my choice how I want to live with the beliefs and stories created in my mind from it. It is my choice if I want to use it as a reason to fail my way through life or deal with it and let it go.

It wasn't my fault I was in a relationship with a drug addict or in a relationship with a drunk that was vile to me. But it was my choice to stay with them and enable the behaviour. It was my choice to believe that I wasn't worth more.

So you see, you can't spend your life blaming and complaining or you will never take charge of your choices and habits. You will never take ownership of your life as you will always seek out someone or something to blame.

You cannot grow as a person while you are still relying on others to bring you happiness and fulfilment. It doesn't work. Please trust me on that. It is a recipe for unhappiness.

Of course, people can enrich your life and you can have good times, but if your happiness is totally reliant on them and their friendship or partnership, then what happens when they mess up? Which people do. You will be so affected by it, rather than realising it really doesn't matter because you are so happy and content with who YOU are that no one can affect that, and you can move on, or just forgive and move forward without resentment.

The biggest lesson I have learned throughout my transformation is that self-love is key. It rules. Once you love yourself so much for the unique and amazing human you are, you can literally achieve anything.

I invested time and money in changing my life for the better as I was so sick of being stuck as the person I used to be.

I have created new ways of thinking and developed an understanding of myself and my thoughts. I can identify what is holding me back and why.

I have already helped so many women begin to change their lives and I am so darn proud of them. It makes my heart burst with happiness when I see the transformations unfold and I watch these beautiful souls go from lost, depressed and stuck in ruts to found, happy and beginning to live life with purpose, gratitude and faith.

When you help someone release thought patterns that have been trapping them all their lives it is like watching a beautiful bird be set free to finally stretch their wings after years of captivity.

I am found. I am home. I am me.

Lots of Love and Courage

Lindsay Nash

xx

ABOUT THE AUTHOR

LINDSAY NASH

Lindsay Nash is a Transformational Life Coach and single mum to five amazing children.

This is her story about how she went from a shivering wreck with no confidence, zero self-esteem, and a belly full of fear and anxiety to a woman with direction, passion, knowledge, and a fire in her belly to help as many women as she can to transform their lives.

Lindsay understands that life wears us down. It can be tough. So learning skills to enable you to cope with the lumps and bumps along the way is key to living a life free from anxiety and turmoil. A life where you have a true understanding of who you are and are super proud of yourself. A life where you are full of confidence in your own actions as you are not ruled by your limiting beliefs.

As a mum Lindsay knows she is her children's role model and how she lives her life will largely determine how they live theirs. For that reason, Lindsay wanted to get out of the mess her life had gotten into and show them how to live their best lives and become the best humans they can possibly be. She wanted to show them how to have courage and resilience and to love who they are so they are able to navigate their way through problems in a healthy and positive way.

Lindsay now helps other mums live happier and more confident lives so that they can inspire their children to do the same.

Lindsay knows that once you change your life for the better it has a ripple effect across your whole family's lives and you will leave an amazing legacy that will continue to shine through future generations.

I dedicate this chapter to my five beautiful children that amaze me on a daily basis with their strong characters and their ability to bounce back from adversity. I am so proud of each of you and without you I honestly don't know where I would be in life. You are my world and the reason why my heart beats, my darlings.
So thank you Jack, Dillon, Finley, Ryder and Oakley for being you.
You are all unique and special. You are all enough just as you are.

All of my Love Forever
Mum x x

Connect with Lindsay at:

Website: www.mumwarriors.com
Email: lindsaynash@mumwarriors.com

facebook.com/mumwarriors
instagram.com/mumwarriors

GUNA RASNACA

THE ROAD TO FREEDOM.

THE INVISIBLE FORCE

y aim is to show you that freedom is available for everyone. No matter what your current and past circumstances are, no matter where, when and to whom you have been born, as long as you are alive, you have the power to set yourself free.

I am someone who has a remarkable willpower, but despite that, until I discovered what the invisible force was that was holding me back, all my attempts to set myself free from what looked like a life-long ongoing struggle were fruitless.

It took me twenty years as I was gathering the knowledge, raising my awareness, continuing to fight, getting up after having fallen and trying again. The drama of my life consisted in serious physical and mental health issues, addictions, workaholism, co-dependency, the pattern of being repeatedly abused, financial struggle, lack of purpose, lack of self-esteem and total inability to love myself.

What once had been a drama turned out to be a success story, once I had stepped out of the victimhood into the growth mindset and fully appreciated how in each misfortune there had been a hidden blessing. From someone deemed to be cursed I turned out to be someone who is extremely lucky. This is not a question of mindset. It is something a tad deeper. Mindset work is going on at the level of willpower and my twenty years of unsuccessful persistence at that level proved that there was some invisible force that was stronger than me.

What was this force? Bad karma, past life, a curse? Or was it me, self-sabotaging in the most subtle and wicked ways? I was swinging between places of victim mentality and willingness to take full responsibility. But this was a challenge for my rational mind, because there were facts. On one hand, I was doing all that was possible with a rare determination; I was a warrior, a survivor. On the other, no matter what I did, there was always something, a sudden obstacle, like bad luck.

As the years passed, I could observe that taking action was definitely not enough. Since I remembered myself, I had been a pragmatic person of action. I was not satisfied with the possibility that it was some invisible external force punishing me for sins that I was not aware of. Even if in deep despair it is easy to adhere to disempowering magical thinking, and I did at times. It was against my belief of inherent goodness of the world.

Similarly, in regards to my health issues I never fully settled with the responses mainstream medicine and science gave me if those were vague, unconvincing and limiting. Like most people in modern society, I was conditioned to believe the conventional experts, but I am glad that my critical mind questioned the diagnoses and treatments when they did not make sense, turned out to be ineffective or worsened my state. When no one could give me an answer that was acceptable and offered long term solutions, I kept searching. And as I did that, inevitably I kept finding many different perspectives, far beyond the limits of modern medicine. I have always believed in causality. And if you believe in causality, you believe that everything must have a solution, even if some kind of supposed authority, like science, does not have it. This is why I never settled.

After a decade of relying on mainstream health care, I spent another decade looking for answers beyond it. Eight years on the psychoanalyst's couch not only saved me from continued medication but opened my eyes to what that invisible force behind all the drama was. So far medication and mainstream therapy (cognitive behavioural) had served only as a band-aid and as years were passing, my unhealed wounds kept growing. But psychoanalysis was an important stepping point that allowed me to access the necessary awareness of the fact that this invisible destructive and limiting force was within. It was a part of myself. It was me, but beyond the self that we can perceive and identify to if we haven't developed a certain level of consciousness.

Even if psychoanalysis had no solution for dealing practically with that force, it had served me to do the foundational work - development of the awareness. I had cracked level 1. I saw my patterns; I could recognise my limiting beliefs; I had learned to investigate down to the root cause; I was now able to outsmart my denial and take the responsibility. However, I still felt helpless as I was facing this invisible power and I had no control over it. My willpower and consciousness were not enough. I felt like a victim of myself. But as I had worked to that level of awareness, the door was open to access the next stage.

I was not the only one who had discovered the limits of mainstream medicine and psychology and I am most grateful to the doctors and scientists who have stepped out of these limits and developed work in fields that carry the explications and solutions that mainstream health care still dismisses. These are fields of trauma, neurosciences, epigenetics, psychoneuroimmunology and quantum physics. The researchers, doctors and scientists who did the work of linking the dots made available the knowledge that is needed to work with that invisible force. They gave me the freedom to choose the freedom.

They lifted the obstacles I had, being someone pragmatic, conservative, and rational, to access the knowledge necessary to be free of the limitations of the conventional approach. Scholars like Dr Bruce Lipton, Dr Gabor Maté, Dr Robert Scaer, Dr. Peter A. Levine and Dr Stephen Porges, Dr David Berceli, Dr Melanie Salmon, just to name a few who played a significant role not only in showing the way to freedom but even saving my life. What they have done in essence was to give the knowledge and tools that allowed me to work with that invisible force. Knowledge that allowed me to release my inner limitations at the level of the subconscious mind and body. I had the confirmation of my experiences that were showing links between body, mind and spirit, the necessity of a holistic approach, and the common denominator of all my issues – the trauma and resulting subconscious limiting beliefs. When I learned and experienced that there was a way to set myself free, it became my mission. I had to spread the word and help everyone else to liberate themselves from the invisible force holding them back.

Freedom starts within. I discovered that it was impossible to be free at the level of physical realities like relationships, substances, medicine, financial and work situations unless I was free within.

I had been "decluttering" my life, letting go of relationships, things and situations, but there was one thing I could not separate myself from – it was me. I was in control of everything, except my subconscious mind. The programmes and limiting beliefs that were seated in my subconscious mind were more powerful that the illusory sense of control and free will. My reality, which felt like a curse, was a reflection of my subconscious beliefs. I could not see why I had such a self-destructing subconscious mind. I discovered that what seemed self-destructing were outdated programmes that were only trying to protect me. My subconscious mind was doing what it is supposed to do and it continued to play out outdated coping mechanisms.

I ended up managing to quit the drama and fully reverse it into a success story of a life with purpose, love, health, abundance and freedom just by breaking out of the prison of my limiting beliefs. That invisible force was my own subconscious mind.

Freedom is when you can be the creator of your life, not a victim of some invisible force or yourself. It is when I set myself free from the prison in the form of my limiting beliefs caused by unresolved trauma. My main obstacle to freedom was the denial and disconnection from myself that was rooted in fear. My victim mentality was rooted in blaming, disempowerment and labels that are used in modern medicine. The lack of awareness concerning my true story and losses that kept me stuck with suppressed grief, was showing up in the form of depression. The lack of knowledge about the subconscious mind, the memory, body and mind connection and trauma. And ultimately my inability to love. I will share my story of overcoming these obstacles and my experiences of life that offered me this particular path.

UNCOVERING THE TRUE STORY; FROM DENIAL TO DRAMA; THE WORK TOWARDS FREEDOM

It is rare to hear someone saying that his childhood has not been happy. I thought I had a happy childhood, because I had no reason to believe it was unhappy and because what I knew about my childhood was what I was told about it. Turned out I had two childhoods, one before I spent eight years in psychoanalysis investigating it, and another one that I discovered after that process.

These discoveries were a metaphorical opening, owning and cleaning of wounds so that they could heal. But it turned out this process had no practical tools, no "medicine" to heal those wounds. I felt victimised, helpless and in extreme emotional pain as I was left with the unbearable number of open wounds. Because the awareness itself does not bring healing, even if it is a necessary stage to access it.

Toward the end of the analysis, when I was 33, I got two violently painful autoimmune conditions (psoriasis guttate and fibromyalgia). My nervous system could not bear the sessions of reopening the wounds any more, and my immune system got confused. This was how my body was saying no so clearly that I could not deny body and mind connection any more and the existence of re-traumatisation in talk therapy.

I believed I had a happy childhood until I was asked to speak about it. In the beginning, I had just three memories, that all represented events where I was terribly scared and humiliated. I carried out a whole investigation; I questioned my family members, I was looking at my childhood photos, trying to recall moments captured there.

I now had a story of a child who was conceived as her mother had no knowledge about how one gets pregnant. I had been an unexpected and unpleasant surprise. She was eighteen. Labour was so long and difficult that after I was born, she fell ill and was hospitalised, and I stayed in hospital care for my first three weeks. Later she tried to love me, but she was emotionally shut down and unable to attune. My father was gone, serving in the army before I was born. I was abandoned physically in the very beginning and emotionally forever. She took care of my physical needs, by the book.

It was early ingrained in my subconscious mind that I was a burden and that I was unlovable. As a survival strategy, I developed a high capacity to read and meet others' needs. I was in circumstances where my survival depended on my capacity to people-please. I knew that it was not safe to be who I was, so I became who I was expected to be. I had no sense of self-worth. During the past ten years I was uncovering and learning to acknowledge the reality of not knowing who I was. And in the past two years, I have been discovering who I am. In a way, I was born when I was 35 years old. This is another dimension of the freedom this story is about, the freedom to be me.

As a three-year-old I was trained to take care of myself so that my young parents who were studying and working could rest. Those sole three memories I had initially were from traumatising events involving my parents losing control, making me feel terrified and humiliated. They did not do it against me, they just acted out what was unresolved within themselves.

When I questioned my parents and other family members about my childhood, they all candidly told me about several events that were emotionally violent and neglectful. As they were sharing memories it was clear that they had no consciousness of the trauma such situations create; it was a normalcy to them. I could tell they felt like they were sharing happy childhood memories. They believed it too. One of these treatments was that I was not allowed to cry, because that disturbed them, so when I was upset, I was sent away to cry in another room. I can't blame them. I understand now. I can clearly imagine myself repeating all the same patterns if I had not done all the work to uncover the true childhood story, to heal from trauma and recover my true self.

No parent harms their children intentionally, they just do what they know to be right and they can only give what they have. Hurt people hurt people. They can do that from a place of lack of awareness, as they live covered by thick layers that keep them as disconnected from their true self as I once was. And I too have hurt many people in the past from my own unconsciousness. I know that my mother, my stepfather and my father are decent people and they tried to do their best, they provided what they could. They were young and each one of them had their own background that explains their limits. They wanted to give me the best, and they did give the best they had. I got an education, I could ski and play tennis, I could have private lessons in English. They were not wealthy, but they gave me what they could afford and what they valued, that was a form of love.

However, the form of love I was longing for was in kind words, care, touch, the one that can be felt, one they didn't know how to give, just like me until I healed and learned to find love within. Emotional attunement was something they had not had themselves as their parents had survived Soviet occupation and genocide against Latvians and carried their own load of unresolved trauma. I was the lucky one who got to break the cycle.

Developmental trauma did turn me into a child who had no one to go to, a child who would not go to her parents in case of a problem. I was on my own since the beginning. A deeply rooted insecurity was installed in my subconscious mind. I learned to take care of the emotional needs of the adults, to please them and to be invisible, not to bother them. I unconsciously kept on doing this in my adulthood. I always felt a need to apologise for everything, almost to apologise for existing. Playing a role, self-neglecting and behaving as expected was exhausting work. It was my unconscious way to try to earn love as I had this deeply rooted belief that I was unlovable.

Abusers typically sense and intuitively approach the type of children who carry that vulnerable energy, who have no one to go to, be it a bully in school or a paedophile like it was in my case when I was five. That was a memory that surfaced working with a psychoanalyst when I was 33. I questioned my parents. No, they did not know. They had no ability to notice my terror and I probably hid it, not to bother them.

On the surface level there was a tale of a happy childhood where I was described as a very easy, obedient child, who enjoyed dancing and drawing, who was getting along with everyone, had no major problems and was a perfect child. Nothing, except my hunched posture that I can see in my childhood photos since I was around five, betrayed my emotional state of fear, shame and guilt. My parents were very ashamed of my posture and tried to correct it violently, pulling my shoulders back and relentlessly reminding me to hold a straight back, with little success even if I desperately tried to please them. My body was not going to lie. As an adult, I continued that unsuccessful fight with the help of physiotherapy, with minimal success until my posture finally transformed after I started to work on my trauma and to practise trauma release exercises.

I lived in the illusion of the happy childhood story until ten years ago when I started to work with an analyst and gradually linked the dots. I started it as prior to that I had been, for more than ten years, seeing mainstream therapists and psychiatrists without success.

At the age of fifteen I told my parents that I was depressed. I was told off; it was not possible; I had no reason. It made sense. I was left alone with it. I believed I had no reason as well, so I just went on with my life, coping as I could, partying, smoking weed, taking other drugs, having sex, going to school, snowboarding like crazy.

Next thing was my first suicide attempt. I was sixteen. I still had no official reason to be depressed, but I now was officially depressed. My passage in the psychiatric hospital was traumatising, and it was something shameful as well, not for me, for my parents.

When mental health professionals first saw me, I had no trauma "to declare", at least nothing that I was aware of or able to express at that time. They concluded that chemical imbalance simply caused my depression and anxiety. So, a molecule would do it. Antidepressants, tranquillisers and sleeping pills never really worked as they made me feel high, unnatural, and spaced-out. Doctors tried different molecules, but it was just worsening my state. Ten years later I was diagnosed with bipolar disorder. It made sense. I had been having suicidal thoughts, depression and anxiety since I was fifteen, I had attempted suicide already twice, and despite that, I had had a life, I had a degree, a career, I had followed my dreams and moved to France.

As I uncovered my true story, I understood that moving to France was rather escaping from pain than following a dream. In reality, I just had moved far away from all the events I subconsciously wanted to forget. Living in another language was therapeutic. However, it is easy to cast someone as bipolar; it is enough to have several breakdowns, chronic depression and high drive for life. I was lucky because three months later I started dating a man whose mother was a psychoanalyst who met me, evaluated me, was scandalised by this diagnosis and spoke to me about neuroses and trauma. Since then I was out of the grip of conventional health care for good.

After childhood followed turbulent adolescence. I was absolutely free to do what I wanted. I guess I had learned to please my parents to the extent that they believed I was a good, serious girl and there was no need to control me, and they were young and busy with themselves. In reality, I was an insecure teenager who was appreciated by all as I was internally broken and big in people-pleasing. I was friends with everyone. I was part of many different groups of friends. Looking back, I can tell I was longing for connection, but I was unable to be close. That was the reason for having so many relationships.

My mother had had the painful experience of having her life disrupted by having me because she had no access to any sexual education, as in the Soviet Union sex did not exist. So, when I had my first period, she gave me a next day pill and instructed me to take it in case I would get raped, so I don't get pregnant.

At fourteen I was partying and the first time I got drunk I lost my virginity, just because I had no concept of saying no. Two weeks later, I was so drunk in another party that I lost consciousness and got raped in front of that group of friends. I was slut-shamed. I felt shame and guilt, I blamed myself for getting drunk. My friends had been there; it was me or them. It was natural for me to take the blame on myself rather accuse them of rape. I was alone. I could not afford to lose them. The guy who did it was the brother of a friend of my parents. I could not do anything about what had happened. I buried it deep down. I wanted to forget.

It is interesting how memories work. There is explicit memory - all that we can recollect. And the implicit memory: all that we remember unconsciously, which has been stored in our body and subconscious mind, things we can't remember but only decode if we desire to do so by careful investigation of our reactions, health, patterns, relationships and limiting beliefs.

After many years of inquiry, it turned out that I had many reasons to be depressed and anxious. It turned out that while my explicit memory had a story of a happy childhood, my implicit memory carried all the reasons for my depression and anxiety. No surprise that no molecule was able to heal beliefs that were clearly not created by a chemical imbalance but by trauma. As it often is with trauma, our brain protects us from memories that are too difficult to deal with. Many traumatic events come with a sense of shame and guilt so that even if we have a recollection of the event, we tend to minimise the impact of it. It is a coping mechanism to suppress, rationalise and trivialise things that have traumatised us if we are alone and have no way to work with it. This is how we survive but as well we keep trauma stuck in the system without even realising it.

One trauma had led to another. I was a textbook case of complex trauma. My subconscious mind was loaded with limiting beliefs that came from my experiences. My vibration was one of a vulnerability that attracted abuse despite me. That was that invisible force in action. At the age of 25, I was sexually assaulted again. By the age of 35, I had had five unsuccessful relationships, all built on foundations of co-dependency, where unsurprisingly I suffered violence and emotional neglect.

From someone who came from a happy childhood, I turned out to be someone who has an ACE (Adverse Childhood Experiences) score of four. The ACE Study is a ground-breaking study conducted in 1995 that has shown that there is a direct link between childhood trauma and adult onset of chronic disease, as well as depression, suicide, being violent and a victim of violence, increased risk of health, social and emotional problems, and that people usually experienced more than one type of trauma – rarely was it only sexual or verbal abuse. Just as this study had shown with the childhood trauma score I had. I was checking all the boxes of the risks they had found were high in such cases. I had alcoholism, I was a smoker, I had chronic depression, I was later raped, I attempted suicide, I had had intercourse by the age of fifteen, my work performance had been impaired, and I had chronic bronchitis. The good news is that since I have healed the trauma, for more than two years I have been addiction-free, mentally and physically healthy and haven't attracted any form of violence or abuse. This is my message: no matter what we have been through and to what we are predisposed, we can heal and set ourselves free.

In the same way, like there was this split between how my childhood looked and how it had been in reality, there was the same pattern in my adulthood too. On the surface I had it all together and was the one that we call a high achiever and high functioning addict. I had got two master degrees, one in Law and the other in Conference Inter-preting. I had tried four different careers with success, but I felt unfulfilled. I had moved countries four times. I was a snowboarder, a surfer, I was living by the beach, always going after my dreams. While at a deeper level, I had no self-esteem, I had suffered emotional and physical abuse in relationships. I was fighting with several addictions. I was regularly burned-out. Being an adrenalin junkie, I was often injured from accidents from wakeboarding, snowboarding and surfing. Anxiety, depression and suicidal thoughts were always present. My PMS used to be the peak of those thoughts and the pain I used to suffer was stronger than any painkillers. I was deeply unhappy, enslaved to my self-destructive patterns and helpless facing self-sabotage. I was not free.

I had worked my way through the denial into awareness, but I was still lacking the knowledge about trauma work, about ways to work with the subconscious mind. I tried and applied all that was promising to heal me, starting from Ayurveda, Chinese medicine, energy work, body-work, yoga (pranayama, meditation), nature therapy, pet therapy, swimming, aromatherapy, lithotherapy, fasting, different diets and tapping.

I was still stuck in victim mentality. I was looking for healing outside of myself. I was there like a beggar, disem-powered, turning to everyone, asking please, help me, please heal me. That invisible force was still in charge. My drama was escalating, and I lost the ability to work. I had left all emotionally abusive relationships behind me to find myself alone. I had fallen into despair. After having thought that this was it, that life was finished for me, that I had failed at everything, that my life was a waste and I had been a lost cause, that there was no hope, I woke up at a hospital after a failed suicide attempt at the age of 35 years.

My life really started that day. I managed to convince the psychiatrist to let me leave the hospital. I knew I was given another chance and I developed a plan of recovery. I combined all I had learned so far and added trauma release exercises. I isolated myself and worked through my withdrawal, as for the first time when I was doing trauma work, I was able to get off of alcohol, cannabis and cigarettes and since then I have never had any cravings. I was working through grief as well. Within two months I knew that trauma release exercises were lifesaving as they had such impact on my nervous system that my immune system was getting close to homeostasis as the symptoms of fibromyalgia had almost disappeared.

As I saw the transformation of my state, I knew I had to spend the money that was left to train in this modality as I was thinking about all those who were living with these conditions believing that there was no solution. I was inspired and motivated. I found a trainer I wanted to train with. She was a medical doctor, who had done case studies with cases similar to mine, and this is how I found the missing piece to accessing freedom. Dr Melanie Salmon had developed a modality that was designed to release limiting beliefs from the subconscious mind.

I recovered in less than a year from what I had been suffering almost a lifetime. I am grateful I survived until I found a way to heal. Trauma work at the level of the body and subconscious mind did what therapy and allopathic medicine had failed to do. This work liberated me from depression, anxiety, addictions, co-dependency, somatic symptom disorder, psoriasis, fibromyalgia and pattern of repeated abuse. I spent twenty years searching, struggling and surviving. Now I am here to show others the shortest way, as my greatest gift was hidden in my deepest wounds. I have found myself, the freedom and my purpose.

Before I could access the tools that are based in activation and used for our individual inner capacity to heal, I had to gain the awareness. To link all the dots, to learn all about trauma, to learn all about the connection between trauma and mental health and the link between mental health and physical health so I could appreciate the holistic trauma healing that consisted of trauma work on the body level and on the subconscious mind level. That awareness was the first stage.

Next stage was stepping out of victimhood into growth mindset that allowed me to take the responsibility and shift from a place of begging for help into self-empowerment where I started to help myself. Hippocrates has stated it already: "The natural healing force within each of us is the greatest force in getting well." Once I had started helping myself actively, people and modalities that were able to support trauma healing started to appear on my path. As I asked for and accepted help from a place of empowerment, I unlocked the door to freedom. The formula was: awareness, intention and work. The tools existed: they were just waiting for me to be ready to use them.

The work takes place within and it is moving through grief to be able to move towards love. I found love for the first time in my life - I found it within. I expressed the love and care I had been longing for, for so long, to myself. Love was my healer, not modalities, not people who supported me through my healing, not myself. The healer was universal love that is born within us and that is mirrored back to us when we radiate it outwards. Love is the one that allows us to move out of victim mentality, as compassion stems from love and it replaces blaming self and others. Compassion replaces self-pity. I had bypassed the grief and so I could not access the bliss. I was in the prison of fear and I could not access the love. The work I had to do was the grief, letting go, losing the fear and accessing love and bliss.

I TAKE THE ROAD EVERY DAY AGAIN AND AGAIN.

What brought me to freedom from the mental and autoimmune conditions I had had previously is that I kept searching, trying and moving despite the fact that so often no one understood, believed and supported me. Honesty, courage, idealism and trust in the highest good kept me from buying into mainstream belief systems. I believed that there must be a solution when the experts said that there was not. I tested and practised all the tools I found. I combined and applied all that I found: diets for gut health, food supplements, Ayurveda, aromatherapy, lithotherapy, breathwork, yoga, tapping, nature therapy, animal therapy, journaling, meditation, chanting, dancing, swimming, walking, self-massage, Pilates, living accordingly to the moon calendar; it all was a part of my road, but what made the difference and allowed me to access the freedom was trauma and tension release exercises and quantum energy coaching combined.

At times it was necessary to make difficult and terrifying decisions to let go of people and things. I took huge scary risks and those were the decisions that triggered the shifts and made new openings and opportunities. Each time when important shifts took place there were challenging periods in between stages. Those periods feel like the time has stopped and you are stuck in between, having left the old while the new is not quite there yet. Sometimes that felt like having lost the ground under my feet, but I knew I must keep moving even if I didn't see what was in front of me: there must be something. I trusted that if I kept moving, I would bring myself somewhere. I went through tough but necessary times of isolation and solitude until new people and things came into my life that was aligned to my new positive beliefs about myself and the world.

I found effective support in people who had been through similar situations and who were teaching from experience, not textbooks. I worked with practitioners who walked the talk. That was what made the difference.

I respected the fundamentals of healing, as I kept on moving my body and moving my imagination to keep both alive, as these are the key elements to life. I want to emphasise that the function of imagination is as important as body function.

I took months to grieve. I practised and I keep practising *Metta* (loving-kindness) meditation and applied *Metta* in form of massage to learn to love and generate the love within.

I learned that it is never too late to quit surviving and to start living as long as you are alive. I am grateful to myself that I never settled when mainstream health care was writing me off with diagnoses of supposedly incurable disorders like bipolar, psoriasis and fibromyalgia. Even if I gave up a few times, I got up and kept on searching for healing, for freedom, for life. After twenty years of searching and experimenting, I found access to freedom. I discovered that it is a never-ending road that I choose to take every day. Just like we choose to love someone every day.

I am now medication free and 100% healthy. What was a drama turned out as a success story that brought me my greatest gifts: freedom, purpose and love. I have learned to love myself unconditionally. I am grateful for each moment of my past as now I see the bigger picture. One thing leads to another. My experience made me; my path was the road to myself. I am glad I took it, and I keep on taking it. As I kept moving until I reached the light, I have now been given the chance to hold the hand of others on that road to freedom. My greatest gift is that I now have the chance to witness others experiencing liberation from conditioning, labels, from limitations, from pain. To see in the eyes of my clients the light of love rising.

Each of us has a unique path, according to the individual's background. We have different resiliency, different coping mechanisms and different levels of sensitivity. What is traumatising for one is not traumatising for someone else. I want to emphasise how important it is to validate your own experience and feelings. Comparison is a source of a lot of unnecessary suffering. The only person you should compare yourself to is yourself yesterday. This is how you stay on the path of growth.

The path towards freedom is a never-ending road of a life-time, a constant moving through layers, accessing higher, and higher stages. Beings like Buddha and Jesus, who had accessed inner freedom, must serve to us as inspiration to thrive towards. This is to say that the learning, the work and the growth never end as long as we are alive, so let's make the best use of the time we have in this beautiful world. We are naturally gifted with the creative force of love and the fun part of life is that we get to create ourselves continuously. Many thousands of years ago already Ayurveda defined that one of the reasons for disease is stagnation. The message is: grow or die. This is why struggle and trauma is a natural and necessary part of life that has a goal: to provide us with lessons and circumstances to expand our resiliency, our heart and spirit. It is safe to drop your fear, to lift the denial and look into a true version of your own story, with compassioned honesty and loving curiosity. Make that first step to take the road to freedom!

Enjoy your journey and remember:

- All you need to get there is awareness, intention and work.
- You are in charge as the only invisible force is just your subconscious mind and limiting beliefs.
- Be effective and work on the cause of your issue instead of the consequences.
- It is not necessary to be able to recall the trauma to be able to heal it.
- It is never just in your head. What is in your head is in your body and what is in your body is in your head too.
- Your body can't lie; your mind can.
- It is necessary to isolate to grief, but don't walk alone. You are ready to get back on the road when you are ready to take the hand that someone is giving you.

- It is possible to leave all abusive relationships except the one you have with yourself, so working on your subconscious mind and body is the priority.
- The only healer is love that is born in your heart.
- It is never too late.

ABOUT THE AUTHOR
GUNA RASNACA

Guna is a Post-Traumatic Growth Coach. She is passioned about growth mindset and healing the root cause of most ailments – chronic stress and trauma at the level of body and subconscious mind.

She has supported her clients on their way out of depression, anxiety, addictions, abusive relationships and autoimmune diseases by working with simple and complex trauma at the subconscious mind and body level.

Her path to trauma work was set out by her studies and experience of twenty years when she faced the limits of modern medicine, psychology and even traditional medicine to heal from her own complex trauma. When she found the way to recover from illnesses that resulted from CPTSD (complex post-traumatic stress disorder) from childhood trauma, sexual abuse, physical trauma and narcissistic abuse, in less than a year, she knew that her mission was to help others. For twenty years she was a functioning serial addict; her addictions included smoking, alcohol, drugs, sex and sugar. She suffered from many psychosomatic disorders, and in her early thirties she developed fibromyalgia and psoriasis. Now she is pain and addiction free, and addiction work and autoimmune conditions have become her main subject.

She strongly believes that anyone who is willing to be free and to heal can do it. She supports individuals in taking back the responsibility and response-ability for their health by doing the trauma work.

She provides trauma healing in a holistic and gentle way to release limiting beliefs fast and permanently. To achieve that she combines Quantum Energy Coaching (QEC) and Trauma and Tension Release Exercises (TRE). She is a Hatha Yoga teacher and practitioner of Traditional Thai Massage; her approach is as well influenced by Ayurveda.

The importance of autonomy and self-empowerment in the healing process is why QEC and TRE are her main tools and why she calls herself 'an assistant of self-healing'. As she assists the process of your self-discovery, self-creation and self-healing she ensures safety, understanding, support and empowerment.

EMAIL: guna.rasnaca@gmail.com
WEBSITE: www.gunarasnaca.com

f facebook.com/gunarasnacacoaching
instagram.com/guna_rasnaca
in linkedin.com/in/gunarasnacacoaching

JANNINA BECKETT

THE STRENGTH WITHIN

> *Anyone can give up; it is the easiest thing in the world to do.*
>
> *But to hold it together when everyone else would understand if you fall apart, now that is true strength!*

— CHRIS BRADFORD

Thank you so much for being here. I am truly grateful that you have picked up this book and turned over the page to my chapter. I feel genuinely blessed to have manifested such an incredible opportunity to allow myself to be vulnerable, share some of my experiences, and reach out to the incredible women that may just need to hear from me today.

It has taken years to truly understand the person I have become, and wholeheartedly embrace the uniqueness and magic hidden deep within me. Having spent so much time challenging my purpose in this crazy, ever changing world, and wondering what legacy I would leave behind, I have found clarity amidst the confusion, learnt the true meaning of inner strength and what it means to pursue my dreams.

> *You are the only one who gets to decide what you will be remembered for!*

Taylor Swift

It's easy to get caught up in the chaos of life, drifting wearily through each day without really being present, and putting everyone's needs before your own, but there comes a point when you just know you are capable and worthy of so much more. It took me a long time to learn what it means to prioritise myself and even consider pursuing my dreams. I realised it wasn't selfish, it was a necessity. It's all too easy to feel guilty for wanting more out of life, but it is even easier to be judged for wanting more. We only get one chance at this life; there are no rewinds. We owe it to ourselves to follow our dreams, to keep going despite other people's negativity and ultimately stay true to ourselves.

> *What's the greatest lesson a woman should learn?*

That since day one she's already had everything she needs within herself.

It's the world that convinced her she did not.

— RUPI KAUR

As a Mindset and Manifestation Coach, I am passionate about helping women to transform their mindset, prioritise themselves and manifest the life they desire. One thing I am particularly passionate about is helping empower women to create flow, joy, and alignment in their lives. I haven't always had the best relationship with myself; in fact, I have been on THE most amazing personal development journey to get to this point. I have learnt to believe in myself and my worth, know that I can achieve anything, glow with self-love and become a magnet to good vibrations. Our thoughts, beliefs and energy create our reality: therefore if you are holding on to a lot of negative beliefs and self-doubt, you will struggle to find personal alignment and flow, and ultimately to manifest the life you desire.

My decision to train as a coach in addition to maintaining my legal career has been hugely influenced by my own journey of self-development and learning to love myself again. Having worked for several law firms before founding my own firm, I experienced immense challenges resulting in extreme low self-esteem and loss of confidence. My mental health suffered, and I didn't recognise myself any more. Learning to love myself was, by far, the hardest part of my journey. The constant self-criticism and feelings of guilt to even consider putting myself first, coupled with criticism, doubt and negativity from others just had to stop. I knew I needed help and I knew I needed to do something… and this is when my whole life started to change!

> Sometimes I wish I could just rewind back to the old days and press pause… just for a while.

— UNKNOWN

I had an incredible childhood and never went a day feeling unloved by my parents. I was always encouraged to follow my dreams and reach my true potential. Not much has changed. My parents are still two of my biggest supporters and are always there to offer advice, support, and unconditional love.

Throughout my school years I was a happy, confident, self-assured child, and had no reservations when it came to putting myself forward in tasks and taking to the stage to share my passion for music performance. As my school years progressed, my confidence and self-esteem grew. This is certainly not how I remember my early adulthood.

Although unsure where life would lead me, I see now how determined I was to make the most of every day. I was destined to be a leader and to help, inspire and encourage others. I sometimes wonder what it would be like to turn back the clock and just be that girl again, before adult life took hold; to experience that unwavering self-belief and unshakeable confidence. Sometimes when I feel my confidence and self-esteem need a boost, I set time aside to visualise the girl I once was and use her to inspire and energise me. How would she feel right now and how would she handle situations that I face daily? She was a little warrior and so determined... and the best part of all... she is still here... inside of me, screaming at me to keep going, be true to myself and follow my dreams. I can hear her now as I write my chapter... I'm here... I'M HERE!

I don't know about you, but sometimes the constant pressure and hustle and bustle of daily life can be exhausting. I often wish life would just slow down, take a pause and allow me to breathe. As women we are constantly trying to be all things to all people, so much so that we often reach burnout. I found myself close to burnout so many times and didn't understand that I had the power to change that until I started to work on myself. This is when I discovered self-care.

Self-care isn't about buying nice things or going out every week, self-care is about taking time away from the stresses of the day to draw lines in the sand, to decide where our limits are and to not exceed them. This isn't just a new trend in feeling good, it's a way to protect our physical wellbeing and emotional health from the dangers of exhaustion. Self-care is about being as kind to ourselves as we are to others, knowing when our energy is running low, taking a step back and replenishing our resources, rather than allowing them to drain away.

The self-care journey takes effort and commitment. Our daily lives can often be fuelled by negativity and stress, so it's more important than ever to take time out for ourselves, and more importantly not to allow guilt to creep in. Never feel guilty for taking time out for yourself, even if it's just enjoying that morning cuppa on the patio outside and listening to bird song or the wind in the trees.

My journey of self-care has taught me to be kinder to myself, to celebrate myself, to forgive myself and ultimately to nurture myself by using a variety of fabulous and life changing techniques, tools and resources which I picked up along the way.

Learning to journal has been one of the most powerful tools in my self-care toolbox, particularly when I feel unsettled or foggy. I often take time to write about what is going on in my head without judgment, shame, or guilt and then I forgive myself for feeling that way. I've found it useful to let go of the emotions attached to people or sometimes situations that haven't served me, and I forgive and give thanks for the lesson. Another important part of self-care is forgiveness. Forgiveness is so powerful to enable the release of stored negative energy.

The more time I invest in self-care and self-love, the more confident I feel. Confidence brings about resilience to the stresses and strains of daily life. I found the more confident I felt, the more I started to put myself out there and try new things, such as writing articles and collaborating with incredible women such as my co-authors in this book. Self-care transformed my life!

> 66 *We all have an unsuspected reserve of strength inside*
>
> *that emerges when life puts us to the test.*
>
> — ISABEL ALLENDE

Having spent seven years studying, sitting exams and training to become a solicitor, I expected that once quali-fied I would feel complete. Just the idea of telling people what I was going to do for a living gave me a warm fuzzy feeling and an immense sense of pride. I had never consid-ered myself to be particularly academic, so the fact that I had graduated from University and Law School with envi-able grades left me feeling joy like I had never felt before. The reality within the profession for me, however, was far from a dream and often felt like a recurring nightmare.

The legal world is renowned for being a man's world and most definitely not a place for a woman who can think and speak for herself, let alone wants a family as well as a career. I considered myself lucky enough not to have expe-rienced much of this type of discrimination but instead became a magnet to negative people and negative opinions.

I started my legal career as a receptionist and worked hard to climb the legal ladder. Over the years, as I progressed and worked hard to better myself, I suffered a barrage of criticism for just being myself. The criticism came from employers and employees alike... "Who does she think she is?" ... "She's really changed!" ... "She thinks she is better than everyone else now!" ... "She'll be after your job next!" ... I think you get the idea. To be kind and caring meant weakness. To have dreams and goals meant you were overstepping the mark and getting ideas above your paygrade. I soon realised that their behaviour was merely a reflection of how they felt about themselves and had little to do with me. Perhaps my passion and energy to succeed, to take risks and to better myself was a threat and intimidating to those who were unhappy with their own lives. I refused to change and no matter how many times I returned home in tears, I was determined to stay true to myself.

I moved around local firms, following new opportunities and the promise of a better career/work life balance, but nothing really changed. Different firm, same old negativity; same old pressure to become something I was not. I committed to more studying and took on working in more areas of law but soon came to the realisation that this was it. I reached a point where I doubted whether a career in law was right for me. Could I really spend the next forty years feeling so invisible, unappreciated, and flat every single day? In a word... no! I had invested too much time, effort and money and I refused to accept that this was as good as it got. Did I also mention I can be stubborn when it comes to people telling me what I will and won't do? No? Well I can!

I continued to work hard, ran myself ragged and worked all hours, with no reward or appreciation, until ultimately, I found a firm with potential. The role attracted a generous salary and kudos. This was it. This is exactly what I had been looking for. My dream job! My new life! I was ready!

Within a couple of months, this dream role became my worst nightmare. The working environment became toxic almost overnight. Few gave me the time of day and those that did had hidden agendas. Female colleagues became difficult to manage and situations were fabricated to humiliate and embarrass me professionally. I was constantly criticised, belittled and told my opinions were unimportant. Support systems were removed and those I should have been able to trust and rely on betrayed me to benefit themselves. I worked hard, but hard work wasn't enough. I had been set up to fail. I was on my own.

I struggled to understand why I was not accepted and why instead of supporting me or trying to resolve any issues, I would instead be criticised, accused of incompetence, or ignored. I stopped believing and trusting in myself. I let the opinions and behaviour of others affect my self-worth.

Having the support of my amazing mum at such a difficult time was invaluable and I will never forget the strength she had, which helped to keep me going and show up day after day. I was under so much stress and pressure that I wouldn't even allow myself to take time off sick. I couldn't sleep, I became ill and my lovely hair began to fall out. I was living a nightmare. I was broken, there was no way out and no end to the misery. I had often wondered what it would be like to start my own firm and do things my way, but how could I? I had little confidence left and I had a family to provide for.

I started to dream about starting up my own firm and even chose the name; a combination of my sons' names, Jayden and Connor, and the formation of Jaycon Legal Solicitors. I had the idea that I could get the ball rolling and work on setting up the firm in whatever spare time I could find. My notice period was rather long, so when the time came, I would tell my employers about my plans, in the hope of being put on garden leave... full pay whilst working on my own business. I had it planned, or so I thought.

Completely out of the blue, I was dismissed, and asked to vacate the building immediately. I was escorted from the premises and my every move to the exit monitored. I felt angry, totally humiliated, and at rock bottom. I experienced waves of panic mixed with relief that my nightmare was over... but this was not how things were supposed to end. I was supposed to have the final word and satisfaction of handing in my notice. I was devastated and didn't know how I would ever be able to recover from this. I experienced panic attacks, anxiety and suffered from depression, worrying about my professional reputation and how I could ever work in law again, let alone set up my own firm. How could I go it alone? I felt useless and incompetent! It was all over!

The tears I cried could have filled an ocean. I was broken and lost. I was stunned with disbelief and wondered why and how this could happen to me. It took a couple of months of feeling sorry for myself to realise there was only one way to go now, and that was up! I grew stronger each day. I received support not only from those around me but from unexpected sources. I was getting stronger, and I was going to show the big players how it should be done!

It would have been quite easy to give up and to spend time going over what happened, focusing on what went wrong, on how unhappy I felt and questioning it all, but instead I chose me. I chose to trust myself and to remember that I am unique, and I am special. Who were they to tell me otherwise? I hated working there and I disliked most of my colleagues. They did me a massive favour. They taught me how not to behave and how not to treat staff. I am now running a successful, award winning law firm, supported by an incredible team of women, where clients seek us out. Those criticisms have become my firm's unique selling points and the reason clients return and recommend us to others.

Staying true to who I am, trusting myself and remembering how unique and special I am have helped me overcome so many difficulties as my career and businesses have progressed. Being ourselves and staying true to ourselves is what makes us who we are. Don't let anyone make you feel guilty for being yourself. Be brave! Take risks! Be your authentic self!

> *Don't worry about the people who aren't happy for you.*
>
> *They probably aren't happy for themselves either.*

— ROSHAN DEEP

Being a woman in business has been immensely challenging over the years and continues to test me on a regular basis, in a variety of different ways. Finding the right people to share in my journey has, by far, been one of the most significant challenges to face and overcome. People I thought were friends have come and gone, people I believed were true supporters and genuinely wanted the best for me let me down. The hard truth is not everybody wants the best for us, and it can hurt even more when it is a friend that lets us down.

I think we can all be guilty of taking negative comments to heart and sometimes it is difficult to understand where they come from. The problem is often rooted in that person's own feelings of inadequacy. They see something in you that makes them feel as though they aren't as good, whether there is truth in it or not, but those feelings are projected through negative thoughts or actions. Instead of dealing with those underlying feelings of inadequacy, it is all too often easier to make snide comments or to insult, which momentarily makes that person feel better, but it doesn't address the underlying feeling of inadequacy and the problem continues. It is important to take a step back and pause. Remind yourself that the problem is theirs and not yours. Their insecurities are causing them to act that way, so try not to take it personally; easier said than done, I know. Taking the pause can help you understand what their behaviour is and help you digest the circumstance.

Being the bigger person can be difficult but gets easier with practice. Words carry power. Being a positive influence in the world is a powerful force. Being a positive influence is what brought about my fascination and interest in coaching.

> Go after your dream, no matter how unattainable others think it is.
>
> — LINDA MASTANDREA

If, like me, you have felt that desire to be more and do more, and really become 'someone', then you need to dream big and pursue that passion. For the most part I have found those around me to be pretty positive and supportive of any dreams and desires I release out into the universe, but it is easy to attract the dream crushers: you know, those people who are going to give you their opinion, whether you asked for it or not. I recently heard such people referred to as 'mood hoovers'. These people seem to have a knack for putting a damper on your ideas, and make you question yourself… and even worse, doubt your dreams. There is nothing worse than sharing your ideas and passion for something, which you feel will be massively impactful, for them to not take you seriously, shut you down or laugh at you for being unrealistic. I have been there. It is not a good feeling and if you are not careful and clear about your dreams, they can really knock your confidence and make you feel alone.

Having clarity on what it is you want to achieve is key, being crystal clear on your dreams, so that when you get knocked down… you are not down for long. I personally find vision boards helpful and lists of what I need to learn, suggestions as to who I might need to reach out to, investments and sacrifices that I may need to make along the way. If you know where you are going, you will be able to stay focused in the face of hardship along the way. The lists and vision board are a great support to motivate and re-inspire you when the chips are down.

I have always welcomed an outside perspective, and have always been gracious when receiving constructive criticism, but it is important to be smart and know how to separate constructive criticism from negativity. I will not let other people's negativity stop me from following my dreams, and I will tell you why; not following your dreams can make you feel unaccomplished and eventually stop you dreaming all together. I am sorry (not sorry) but that is not for me. I know that not taking that chance on myself will fill me with regret and make me question why I didn't do it sooner. The only yes I need to follow my dreams, is my own! It is important that you don't let others define you by telling you who you should be, what you should do or how you should behave. If I had conformed and changed to what others wanted me to become and behaved the way others wanted me to behave, I would have become hard, uncaring, unempathetic and a yes person.

To achieve a dream, you must believe in yourself. I know it sounds simple, but it isn't just the dream crushers we have to watch out for. Sometimes we can be our own worst enemy and can often get in our own way. To be able to achieve our dreams, we must truly believe in ourselves and our abilities. If we don't believe in ourselves, we will lack confidence to follow our dreams. We all have negative thoughts, but it is important to consciously turn them on their head and not empower them. It can be tough, I know. I have often struggled with my self-esteem and my confidence, and there are still days when I find believing in myself harder than others, but I have found ways to rewire my thoughts and alter my subconscious. Journaling can be a huge support in times of negativity and coupled with positive affirmations can help navigate the struggle and provide support in those moments of self-doubt.

The difference between those who live out their dreams and those who don't is action. If it was easy to achieve our dreams everyone would do it. You can dream all you like, but unless you take action, a dream is all it will ever be. I am, by nature, a doer. As a doer, I have the power to create, influence and change everything in my life. I won't say that following my dreams hasn't taken unexpected turns, but it has brought about the excitement and memorable challenges that have come from living my dream. Accomplishment brings about personal satisfaction and sparks bigger dreams. By pursuing your dreams, you are giving hope to others who want to do the same. You can serve as their inspiration and a reason to give something a try. At the end of the day, there are no rules when it comes to your dreams, so why limit yourself?

I have overcome many challenges, particularly in my professional life. So many of those difficulties have pushed me out of my comfort zone and have often been quite uncomfortable and unpleasant at times, but pushing through the discomfort and taking on those challenges can help us grow as women. We become resilient and bounce back even stronger than we were before. Dreams can make you take chances, and chances create opportunities. It's important to grab those opportunities and never let go!

When the opportunity arose to start my own law firm, I was really scared and doubted whether I was strong enough. I chose to embrace the fear and just do it anyway. Similarly, with my coaching business, starting a new venture, having been in law for so long also felt scary, and came with a whole new set of limiting beliefs to overcome.

> *The greatest mistake you can make in life is to be continually fearing you will make one.*

— UNKNOWN

Can following your dreams be scary? Absolutely! Do I pursue my dreams despite the fear? Absolutely! Fear can make you feel more alive. Taking those first steps can be the scariest part, and there will no doubt be sceptics at the side line, reminding you of the risks and reasons not to proceed, but don't let that stop you, because if you don't try then you will never know. Taking risks can help you feel alive, and if you feel alive, you can smash through any fear, especially the fear of making mistakes. Life's greatest lessons are learnt from mistakes but more importantly, mistakes have the power to turn you into something better than you were before. Mistakes are proof that you are trying.

It has only been over the last few years I have realised that the pursuit of my dreams has been the inspiration behind the actions of others. The passion I have for following my dreams has made me interesting, even to people who don't know me. What a legacy! Not only have my dreams given me goals to pursue, and the drive to pursue them, but clarity, focus and fulfilment.

> *Your circle of friends must match your own aspirations and dreams, or you will find little support when you need it most.*

— LEON BROWN

There is no denying the power of being surrounded by likeminded people. People who share your aspirations and dreams, people who are there to encourage, support and reaffirm your desires. I have found over the last few years that I have gravitated away from certain friendship groups and found new connections, connections that come along when you are living in alignment with your dreams. Chances are, you will meet these connections spontaneously, and you will learn and grow, inspired by their influence.

Some dreams take longer than others to achieve, but that's what makes the end destination so worthwhile, and when you are this motivated it is hard to fail. Whatever life throws at you, the decision on how to react in the face of adversity ultimately rests with you. Adversity is not failure. We all have a story of adversity, so expect to be tested but don't confuse adversity with failure. Adversity is meant to make you stronger; failure means giving up.

Know that you have greatness inside of you. You are unique, you are you and once you start believing in yourself and following your dreams, there will be no stopping you. Make that promise to yourself that you will start pursuing your dreams!

Dream big! Focus on your dreams! Make your dreams happen!

> *Never underestimate the power of dreams and the influence in the human spirit.*
>
> *We are all the same in this notion:*
>
> *The potential for greatness lives within each of us.*
>
> — WILMA RUDOLPH

So, as I come to the end of my chapter, I would like to thank you, from the bottom of my heart, for allowing me the honour of your precious time.

My final thoughts to you are these......

Believe in yourself and your dreams!

Don't let the behaviour of others define or destroy your inner peace!

Be you; uniquely you!

ABOUT THE AUTHOR

JANNINA BECKETT

Jannina Beckett is a Mindset and Manifestation Coach, Founder of Jannina Beckett Coaching and Minds-Over Matters Ltd. She is a certified NLP (neuro linguistic programming) and Breakthrough Coach Practitioner as well as a published co-author of a number one best seller for female entrepreneurs.

In addition to her commitment to coaching, Jannina is also the founder of the award-winning law firm Jaycon Legal Solicitors. Jannina's decision to train as a coach in addition to maintaining her legal career has been hugely influenced by her own journey of self-development and learning to love herself again.

Jannina is passionate about helping women to transform their mindset, prioritise themselves and manifest the life they desire. It has taken Jannina several years to truly understand and embrace her authentic self, learn the true meaning of inner strength, and pursue her dreams. Here, Jannina shares parts of her journey, experiences, and the lessons she has learnt along the way.

You can find her at www.minds-over-matters.com

Download her freebie '7 Steps to Transform your Mindset and Manifest the Life you Desire' at

Website: https://www.janninabeckettcoaching.com/
Email – contact@minds-over-matters.com

 facebook.com/mindsovermatterscoaching
 instagram.com/mindsovermattersofficialinsta

KATE BLAKE

I have had my fair share of stress in life.

I was put up for adoption at a week old. I was raped at the age of sixteen. I have lost those close to me. I have suffered with anxiety and low confidence and there have been times that when I have stood still, I have felt silenced by life, I have felt little.

Life is a strange thing. We get such huge highs and some lows that make us wonder, why? I live in a house, I have a job, I have my health. I am really grateful. But even we who live our lives worrying about first world problems, which are generally not life and death situations, have to deal with situations that are at times beyond our control. I'm not talking about "gosh how inconvenient that my avocados haven't ripened in time to put on my salad" problems. I'm talking about the things that affect us all around the world, and all the other bits of baggage we humans create.

There are situations I have dealt with in the past: I have documented previously about my issues with lack of confidence and self-esteem, I have also talked about being raped as a teenager and the spiral downwards that led me in my life and the time it took me to heal. How long it took me to survive such a trauma and how I continually attracted more desperate situations until I had actually addressed my issues. You can read all about my story in my book '*I Will If You Won't Let Me!*'

I have stood at many crossroads. I have looked at each path and not known which one to go down. The time I am going to talk about, took me down a rather unexpected path. It goes to show that at times life can have a very strange and sometimes cruel way to remind you how important it is to value yourself and those around you. But the lessons we learn from these situations can help us grow as people. As caring individuals who then take a path to help and serve others.

I remember the day well. It was a snowy morning and I was sat in the kitchen in a fluffy dressing gown. I was assessing my life. I had certainly had a tough life, like many of us. I had my share of loss and disappointment, in myself mainly. But the thing was, I was at my peak, I thought. I had a well-paid job, I had picked up a fantastic bonus, but I was feeling sad. I couldn't understand why. I was two years away from my fiftieth, and I couldn't help feeling I was being ungrateful, as I was now able to provide well for my family. But this wasn't enough, I wasn't aligned, and I had a feeling deep down my path was to help others. I had no clue how to do this.

I decided at that moment to get help. I was not going to wake up at fifty without making considerable changes. I can only say, this felt so deep, you could say it was almost a calling. I had been following a coach and businesswoman for some time, so I took the plunge and made contact. That call was life changing!

A few weeks later after talking and talking and offloading all my life onto my coach, she asked me a question. "If we removed all the barriers and roadblocks that are stopping you moving forward, what would you do?" I thought about this, and said in a small voice, as I thought she may laugh, "I want to write a book and motivate people to get the best out of their lives." She smiled at me, looked me in the eye and said, "I'm so glad you said that. Let's do this!"

This moment described was me standing at a crossroad. It wasn't the first time this had happened. My earlier life had been full of big situations, from being adopted, being raped, and loss, but in the middle of that, I had seen joy. I had been adopted by a wonderful family, so I had felt love and I understood what that was. So, when I found myself in really tough situations, I was able to dig deep and feel love. I knew even through moments of darkness I was able to draw on this and I was grateful for this.

I had not had the best time at school. I was dyslexic and in the 1980s it wasn't picked up; in fact, it wasn't until 2009 that it was picked up. In my last year of school in 1985, I went to a careers' session. I was sixteen and the lady looked me up and down and told me not to expect much in life. My grades were not going to be good. I knew that and I believed her and for many years I dropped out of life more and more. It wasn't until I came to one of my most powerful crossroads that I turned the tide on this future.

The day this happened, I was around 28. I was sitting on my sofa, and I was crying. I was a skint single mum of two boys, and I had been going down the wrong path for a long time. I felt stuck, sad and at my lowest ebb but as I heard my boys upstairs arguing and fighting, out of the feeling of hopelessness came a feeling of love and hope. It radiated out of me, like a bright light shining from the deep, a glow perhaps, and at that moment, I decided to make the change. Over the next ten years I re-educated, I went to counselling and rebuilt myself and my future. For me and my boys.

So, let's go forwards again to that moment coming up to my fifties when I had just decided to write a book. How did I progress with that? Well, actually the writing came easily. I had a big story and it flowed out of me. But in writing a book I had decided to share my story. This was a story that at times I had been ashamed of. I hadn't done well with education in my earlier years, so when I was bringing up my boys on my own, I set up an escort agency and took up lap dancing to put food on the table. The second activity, I actually had quite a good experience in. However, the first activity led me down a road that wasn't so positive, and I felt haunted by it a long time after I had left the industry. I actually hadn't done anything particularly unethical; however, the whole thing felt totally unaligned with my values.

However, what was important was the way I literally changed my path through education, counselling and coaching. The facts were that for many years I had been on anti-depressants and was self-medicating with marijuana, I had been raped whilst on holiday with my parents and had suffered terrible losses at an early age. I had also struggled with relationships and often felt very alone and sad. But all that changed with a total change of mindset, determination and the love for my children, and the knowledge that I wanted to help others. Again, my thought that sharing my story with others could help them is what drove me forward.

It felt amazing and therapeutic. So, within a few months I had completed forty-two thousand words. This was huge for me. I was able to get the book published by Authors and Co and a few months later I was an Amazon Best Selling Author! Boom! Mind blowing. Believe me, when you write a book, people do think it's a bit weird. I mean, normal people or non-famous people don't do this, and I felt I was viewed as a bit odd for doing it. I imagined associates and family thinking, "What hair brained scheme is Kate up to now?" It's not something many people do, and my life was a little odd at times. But people reacted really well, and I gained a new sense of respect for my story from others.

I featured in the national press and I had people around the world wanting to talk to me. It was amazing. So the next step for me was helping others. I had managed to clock up thirty years of sales experience and customer services in the corporate world and had looked after multi-million-pound accounts. I had also coached on and off within the industry especially within customer service and I had loved that, so coaching was something I felt I would like to do. I knew from my own experience it changed everything.

During the time I was actually writing my book (which at this point I had not discussed with my work), I was at my yearly appraisal at work. You know that moment in your yearly appraisal when your boss asks you, "What do you want to do in the future?" For me this had always been easy. I had always stated that I would like to work towards being a Sales Director which was a natural progression in my career. I thought the title and prestige from the job, as well as a nice pay packet, would be exactly what I wanted and was a natural move. But I had realised over the previous twelve months watching all the sales directors I knew, I would like to do more, something different. It wasn't about title any more, it was about how could I help others.

I knew I had learnt so much over my thirty years of corporate work and I wanted to help others be successful at what they wanted to do. I had always undersold myself and I wanted to help others see their potential. But I loved sales and I did want to continue in my sales position and continue to 'smash it ' or do well in it, but also had a feeling that in the future I wanted to look at helping and mentoring other women, who had possibly had some of the issues I had suffered. I wanted to help and give back in thanks for all those who had helped me along the way.

Now when I mentioned this to my employer and his number 1, I was greeted with, "You can't do that… you're down there, not up here like us!" I was shocked by this and actually didn't know what to say. I'm a very polite person, so although in my head I was thinking, "What an idiot," I politely smiled, thinking, "You're not going to tell me I'm down there and get away with it. No Way!"

I have felt down there when I was face down at the age of sixteen being raped, believe me! When I was lied to and I blamed myself for not being good enough. When I was lap dancing and I was told not to bother educating myself because, "What can you do? You're just a body for us to look at." When I tried to better myself when my kids were young and tried to get a job and was asked, "Are you one of these scrounging single mums we hear about in the newspaper?" So, believe me, I had felt "down there" at times. After years of education, self-development, and struggle to get to that point, the last thing I needed was another entitled middle-aged man telling me I was "down there". I would never tell someone else they were "down there" and I guess I also didn't expect at my age to be hearing those kinds of things either, so I was disappointed in them both. That was the saddest thing for me, that people I respected could have such little respect for me, seeing me as being "down there."

Things took another turn a few months later. I have to say, I wasn't sure how to process my success with my book. I loved the process, but when I became a best seller, I was incredibly humbled and probably didn't shout about it too much. I also started feeling very unhappy in my day job. Although I was performing well and my sales were through the roof, I was being constantly pulled up for the most bizarre things, and I was starting to think my face didn't fit in that organisation any more.

The truth is, I had hit a brick wall; in fact, I had literally smashed into it face first. I have a thyroid deficiency and at that point it was very imbalanced I felt so ill. So, all this time I was still working a day job, and at the beginning of the next year I started to get ill. I had burnt out. Even though I had a new idea in my head about a new future, I had focused and worked so hard on my day job that I had missed appointments with the doctors for my ongoing thyroid issue. Big mistake. I had decided my issue was the menopause, but It was actually burnout and a thyroid issue. I cannot tell you how bad I felt. I also have fibromyalgia, so sleeping was becoming a luxury, I was tired, my head was fuzzy, and I wasn't eating. I felt I was literally walking around with a heavy weight on my chest. Getting up in the morning had become a chore. I felt out of breath, nauseous, dizzy and fatigued. I was keeping up with my job but struggling physically. It was seen in the company that sickness was a weakness, so I kept going. I planned to have a great year in sales and to hit my targets, but deep down I was so poorly, I knew I had to stop. But how do you get off a merry go round that just keeps going? The corporate world is not always great when you are poorly. It's as if you become a bit of a nuisance. Jobs for life seem scarce so there is always pressure and guilt attached to bad health.

I had a rather upsetting meeting with my manager. Although he had told me the previous year, "I was down there," I was now being told, "Who do you think you are?" all because I had written a book. It seemed like a no-win situation for me, so I knew I had choices. That evening I spoke to my brother. He was telling me about his weight loss that he had been struggling with for years and had hit his target. He was really excited, and I just didn't want to take that away from him with my feelings. However, I briefly told him I was having some trouble at work but didn't elaborate. I told him I felt poorly and was going to the doctors. We chatted and he tried to make me feel better and laugh as he always did.

The next day I went to the doctor, I had blood tests etc and I got signed off. I contacted work. I felt like they thought I was crazy. I could just hear them saying, "She's totally lost it." I felt so alone, so sad and was questioning my future. I really wanted to continue doing sales, with the addition of being some sort of coach. I wanted to continue writing and make a future for my fifty plus years, to support others and myself and my future, but what if …? What if I couldn't do it? What if I was down there? I mean, "Who did I think I was?" I felt like I had been pushed back. I had for that moment been changed. I had so much doubt and confusion. All that work I had done felt like it was being taken away from me. What was I thinking? I mean, me an author and coach? Who would want to work with me?

A few months previously I had invested in some training courses, so I kept up with them. These were online coaching courses where I would be in a workshop with other women learning about mindset and coaching. I was showing up, but I really wasn't there. I was taking part, but visibly I had been wounded. But I tried to keep going. In fact, at that time, I didn't realise how important all that work I was doing on the course would be to me.

One day when I was on a call, my husband came upstairs to tell me that the police were downstairs. I told him to tell them I was busy, presuming it was just a local issue, perhaps a car robbery or something, but he said I had to come downstairs.

When I got downstairs in my meek manner, I had decided to show defeat to the world and give in when the two policemen told me sit down. I guess when the police tell you to sit down, you know it's serious.

I couldn't move; I was already broken. What else? What had happened? Straight away I thought about my sons who were grown. "Which one is it?" I demanded as I jumped out of my seat. "Please sit," they said. So, I gave in and sat down. They then asked me if I had a brother and gave me his name. This is where life draws in, it goes slow, like in a movie. It's like you're standing behind a window listening to detail; it's vague detail, but still too much to hear, to understand.

My brother had been driving on the motorway. He had had a sudden heart attack; he had pulled onto the hard shoulder; he had died. It seemed impossible, really, as I had had that conversation with him a couple of days previously. We had discussed his weight loss, and I felt I may not have given him enough of my time, because I had been preoccupied with my work situation. He had texted me saying not to work for psychopaths (good advice there), literally a day earlier. He had been with my son at the weekend buying a guitar. It was shocking, crushing, heart-breaking and also so numbing. Disbelief hung over me. Was this real?

My heart, which was also feeling weak, felt that it may explode. As I took in the details my mind switched to tell me I had a lot to do. I had to be strong, I had to get healthy, I had to look after things. Family stuff, and I was now the head of the family. I needed to support others. It's funny how "Action" comes into play in times of tragedy.

I'm not going to go into all the family stuff, but what I'm trying to tell you is how life throws so much at you in one go. It's very difficult to unpick. But at some point, you decide it's time to be a warrior because if you don't, you are not going to cope.

So, with all this going on, I knew I had to be strong. I was going to be dealing with people I had not seen for a long time, helping other family members and trying to do more than think about how sorry I was for myself. Yes, to some extent the "doing" was making me bury my head, even though the pain and loss of my brother was raw, and yes, it hurt. But I had to get on and do the things that needed to be done.

I also realised at this time, I had to resign from my job. I had had a couple of colleagues really reach out to me, bringing me flowers, but did feel like the company had really washed their hands of me at this point, so I had to do the same. It was time for a change in all areas. I needed to find a more positive and healthy way forward. It actually took feeling broken to realise how I needed to care for myself more.

I was lucky. I had a few saving graces at this time, which were my family: husband, sons, daughter and friends. I felt so grateful for that, as well as the new people I had met in my coaching world.

Surprisingly for me at this time, I had grown my coaching business too, and also had clients to coach. These all appeared out of the blue. I was so grateful for them. Although I was coaching them, they will never know how much they helped me. It was huge. I was able to immerse myself in their requirements during their sessions which was a great focus. I had a responsibility to show up and be the best I could be for them. Sometimes they weren't aware that I would be quickly popping a bit of makeup on and brushing my hair and throwing a shirt on over my pyjamas. Making any physical effort to wash or shower was such an effort. But I would be there in the moment for them. I was learning and reading about positive mindset, and loads of other methodology, which was helping me immensely. The mindset work I had been doing on my courses was taking such a huge place in my life, helping me heal and cope.

My lovely little dog was a huge help. She followed me around all day, watching me and caring. Such a comfort.

The friends I had made in the writing and coaching world also checked in on me daily. They called to make sure I was coping with everything. If you know someone going through this stuff, really, it's so appreciated to get a message or a quick call. Although sometimes I felt unable to talk and people understood this, it didn't stop them checking in by text, sometimes forcing me to do something. Believe me, it's easy to start going downhill fast in these situations. Burying your head and hiding. I wanted to sleep but was suffering insomnia.

But I felt so low when I stopped. I felt like I had a toxic thorn in my heart from my work situation, which almost stopped me from being able to grieve properly. I felt this and knew I needed to grieve and to renew myself. I knew my brother would not want me to suffer.

So, I decided to get some counselling. I offloaded, I really offloaded, and I started seeing light appearing at the end of the tunnel. We discussed narcissists' behaviour at work and how they can be rather sticky and are difficult to let go, and we worked that thorn out of my heart. I could now see that a job is not worth your health. Without our health what do we have?

I had also been advised to have some sound therapy. I had never heard of this and it was with tuning forks. But with an open mind I attended. I have to say I am a total convert to this now. I felt a feeling of hope I hadn't had. Perhaps it was the deep meditative state I entered into;

whatever it was, it was hugely helpful. I would really recommend it.

I was making sure I was eating properly, which was a serious effort at times, but also drinking water. I was trying to take the dog out daily, which was tough because I had felt safe in a cocooned safe place in my house. But I felt slowly that getting some air, seeing the trees and park areas were making me feel more alive again. More in touch with my healthy self.

But I learned with the help of others to cry, really cry. Let it out. Remember wonderful things about my brother, about our relationship. I will always miss him, but his memory and knowing how proud he was of me, how proud he was to be in my book, how proud he would be that I was coaching people and making a difference, has spurred me on. I will honour his memory with the love I give the world and those who are in my life and those who are yet to be in my life.

The whole situation has made me realise how important I am within my family and how precious life is. I made a decision there and then that I would grow my coaching business so I could help as many people as possible. I would also look to create a new life for me, where I could be there for my family. I could work in my own time, building a business around my own values and helping women with my experience. So, Kate Blake Coaching grew. I started being more consistent and honest with people about what I was doing and the experiences I had gone through and not being afraid to show my vulnerability and grief.

As time has gone on, I look back and can still feel all those emotions and the physical pain those situations gave me. I speak to a lot of clients who talk about the toxic workplace. I speak to those who have had loss. I understand, and I listen. That's exactly what I needed, understanding, and people to listen. I visited my bereavement counsellor for a year after my loss. It was so important for me to ensure I was working through the loss with someone. I have to be my best in other areas of my life so holding on to pain is not the best. I've always been one to address my issues, I've realised its best to reach out, and I'm not ashamed of that. I would encourage everyone to do that.

Things happen in life that test our resolve, our faith, our love and our health. I am still healing through this. But my business has actually grown. I have stood in front of audiences and talked about my life. I also have grown in my experience and love for life. I know our time is so precious, so short, we have to grasp it with both hands. We have to cherish the world, our lives, the universe, and each other. I know with the things I have suffered in life, it has made me truly grateful for the good and wonderful life I have, the family, the friends, the people I meet, and the experiences this world has offered me, as well as the things to come. It's our time to glow and we also glow to help each other.

I am now certified as a professional coach and NLP, Hypnosis and Timeline practitioner because I felt that, along with my thirty plus years in the corporate world, it would help me be a huge help to my clients.

I started doing more speaking and group coaching, coaching women all over the world from the UK to Zambia, South Africa, and Dubai.

I've created my signature programme Relight your Life 1-1 Coaching. My six months 1-1 coaching has been so popular, to my intensive six hour programme, and my group sales course which is short and to the point, but has proven very popular with my clients as I take my mindset learnings along with my sales experience to help create a full package of support helping people who like me have found themselves at a crossroad, but who want to improve their career, their businesses or really want to create a new life full of purpose and passion. My programmes are moving online soon too. Exciting times.

As I stand in front of you today, at fifty-one in 2020, the year of COVID and lockdowns, I am actually so excited for my future. I feel stronger, although I'm human, and I still have challenges of course, such as menopause. I could write all day about that! But I see through troubled times there is always hope. We live in a country where we have a choice. We can reach out to find help. We can connect with amazing communities, and we can show love and support to those who are in need.

Coaching changed my life for sure. I never used to invest in myself, unless it was consumables which gave me a five-minute high. But the life learning I have received since working with coaches has been huge. The tools I have learnt, that I equip my clients with, are life changing. My belief that there is more to life than we know has grown. I feel my brother is walking with me every day, helping me.

When I first met my coach, I told her that I felt like I had left things too late, that I had missed the bus. Her answer was, "How have you missed the bus? You have just got on it!" She was so right. My journey has just started. Never think it's too late.

Life will always throw challenges at us. Help, love each other, and step forward with strength and glow.

ABOUT THE AUTHOR

KATE BLAKE

Kate Blake is a Mindset and Business Coach, Author and Public Speaker.

Kate has worked within the corporate world for well over thirty years and created a passion for relationship building and sales, running accounts up to £25 million in the construction industry.

She has worked her way up in sales, working in advertising back in the 1980s, moving into finance and then construction.

In 2018 she released her first book "I Will If You Won't Let Me!" which became an Amazon Best Seller. It has been read all over the world and it follows Kate's story from birth, adoption, low self-esteem, sexual abuse and loss. While working in low paid sales jobs back in the late 1980s and 1990s Kate subsidised her low income by pole dancing, whilst starting her journey in education.

Kate has faced many challenges but shows how she has turned her life around to create a positive surrounding for her children, with love and the wish to be able to help others who may have been facing adversity to see that there is hope.

Education has been a big factor in Kate's life. After struggling at school with dyslexia, Kate spent many years re-educating and advocates continuous personal development. Kate is passionate about helping others to believe that they can change their lives in a positive way at any age.

Kate has been featured in various media publications talking about her experiences, helping others see that positive change is possible. She has featured in The Sun, The Express and The Star and as a contributor for Daring Women Magazine.

Kate is also a Certified Coach, NLP, Hypnosis and Time-line practitioner and brings all her experience to her clients from feeling stuck in a rut and at a crossroad, to create new career opportunities and businesses, and a healthy mindset to help them succeed in creating the lives they desire.

Kate lives in Birmingham the UK and is married with three grown up children and her dog, Jade.

Please see below for ways to contact Kate Blake

Email: kate@kateblakecoaching.com
Website: www.kateblakecoaching.com

instagram.com/Iamkateblake
linkedin.com/in/kate-blake-coaching

"Change is the only constant in life.

One's ability to adapt to those changes will determine your success in life."

— *BENJAMIN FRANKLIN*

The power of mantras. "Health is our greatest wealth" rang true and aligned for me, especially these last few years, so much so that I've been making some pretty significant changes seeking a more balanced lifestyle.

If breathwork is the new yoga, I am progressing in the right direction as this is the latest addition to my healing modalities toolbelt.

As individuals we more often than not fear change rather than embracing it, resisting what's new or different. In everyday life, we tell ourselves false stories all the time, not tuning into our full potential. Breathwork is where that all changes. We allow ourselves to go to our edges to find our centre, by activating parts of our brain or releasing trauma, allowing it to be therapeutic, a consciousness awakening and an immune booster all bundled together.

> "*Listen, are you breathing just a little and calling it a life?*"
>
> — *MARY OLIVER*

We all have stories inside. We suppress them and ignore them if they're too ugly to deal with, but that only causes more harm in the long run. Our growth comes from within. If we are the alchemist of our body, can we make ourselves ill as well as heal?

Rarely do we pull back the layers, allowing ourselves to be seen and reveal the secrets beneath. I could've said the same for myself, but have come to realise that it's those layers and stories which make us who we are today.

The last decade has been tumultuous with significant health problems - miscarriages, divorce, an uncertain few years to follow, a flesh-eating bacteria entering my lymphatic system, sexual assault by a supposed trusted friend of twenty years, finding love, moving countries, a mammoth renovation lasting eighteen months, significant infertility issues, coming to terms with the fact that at best I was going to be a step-mum and not experience motherhood, getting married in Italy and deviating away from my career of 25 years to learn new skills, build my own personal brand online to transform lives through holistic health, personal development tools, manifesting and abundance activation.

> *"The journey into self-love and self-acceptance must begin with self-examination... until you take the journey of self-reflection, it is almost impossible to grow or learn in life."*
>
> — *IYANLA VANZANT*

Growing up I pitched myself as "average". The only thing I ever quoted myself being good at was ballet. I started when I was five and loved it, doing all of the various styles our local dance school provided and was awarded scholarships. In every other way I was average. Average height, looks, academically and in sport.

Back then kids got away with more, calling me Casper for my pale skin, or saying I must've got a tan through the fly screen because of my freckles. I cared more about my big front teeth which made me not want to smile, and of course there's the unavoidable one, my webbed toes! This drew ridicule far and wide, making me an easy target for all sorts of remarks. Even now I still receive that one, but with age comes a level of confidence and different self-esteem priorities.

> *"How many cares one loses when one decides not to be something but to be someone"*
>
> — *COCO CHANNEL*

I did what I could to fit in and looking back, I made no effort with my appearance, hiding behind being a skinny tomboy, dressing casually in oversized clothes and not delving into makeup until my older years. Looking at old photos from that era makes me cringe. I was practically the opposite of the Instagram ready teens you see today, which I am not saying is a good thing either: somewhere in the middle may be best.

A major turning point in my life was when I went to Fiji on a foreign exchange programme for a month and turned seventeen when there. I was a scared little girl crying with fear at doing something on my own and ended up loving the experience so much, I cried when I was leaving to head home again because I didn't want it to end.

That was a genuine revelation for me, demonstrating that great things and experiences can happen if we just take that initial step out of our comfort zone.

Sadly, on that trip I also contracted rheumatoid arthritis. It was excessively hot, my hands swelled and my rings were unable to get past my knuckles. At first the doctors thought it was a parasite from the food or water, since I was consuming all of the local produce with the host families.

My poor parents felt terrible, that they shouldn't have encouraged me to go, but hindsight is a wonderful thing and how were we to know this would be the onset of arthritis at such a young age? I've only recently been told it's likely I was always going to get it, but there must've been an emotional trigger on that trip as the catalyst.

This new information made my mind begin to race back trying to remember the finite details all of those years ago. What happened? What could it have been? I had a cold at the time and had always believed the onset was because my immune system wasn't strong enough to fight both.

During the Fiji trip, there was an incident one night, when everyone was sleeping and I saw the Father (who was also a Doctor) standing in my bedroom doorway. I rolled over to let him know I had seen him, which at the time I thought I had saved myself from something untoward happening. However this may have been a figment of my imagination, perhaps since he knew I wasn't well, he was merely checking on me.

Was that my trigger? The story I had perhaps falsely created for myself and believed all of these years?

I wish I knew.

I completed high school and found employment in the newly emerging IT sector. My health was a low priority. I was taking prescribed steroids and anti-inflammatory medication to slow down the rheumatoid arthritis progression. I took them for years and shunned the advice a naturopath gave me because I was a particularly fussy eater and there was no way I could fathom the regime she advised.

Sorry, Mum, I know you tried.

Instead I absolutely battered my poor body, not acknowledging I was sick or different from everyone else. We were the first year out of school and knew all of the bars that hosted $1 drinks across Sydney. We were out six nights a week, moving from one establishment to the next. Upon reflection, I was abusing my body.

I don't know what my relationship was with self-love back then. I don't think I even acknowledged the concept.

The side effects of the drugs were beginning to impact my body as well. My liver, kidneys, bone density, susceptibility to weight gain, hair growth in undesirable places and the moon shape face feature.

Not great.

A few years later my career progressed, so my boyfriend and I left home to go travelling overseas, using London as a base to work and steppingstone to be able to explore Europe. My older sisters (twins + five yrs) were already over there, which made packing bags and moving to the other side of the world less daunting. I only lasted eighteen months (one winter was enough). It was a fun, crazy time in my life, we made many memories that are fit for reminiscing and fun-filled stories, but still I was careless, not looking after myself and was physically paying the price for it.

I returned to Australia thinking I was older and wiser, but it was still not enough to snap out of it. It was only after noticing the side effects of the steroid drugs impacting my body, I realised it was time to make a change. One of my besties knew a homeopath which was my first introduction into these remedies, opening my eyes to a range of new possibilities

It was a slow painful journey. While I could reduce my daily cortisone amount, when it dropped below 1-2mg, my whole body reacted. I couldn't sleep. My arms felt like burning pins and needles, meaning I would be up walking the floor multiple times a night with my arms swinging as though I was swimming backstroke standing up to get the circulation going again.

This was a particularly tough time, but yet I continued life thinking I was the same as everyone else.

I ended up having both of my hands and wrists operated on for carpal tunnel, also removing synovial fluid from my palms. The doctor told me that they were the biggest bags of fluid he'd ever seen. I felt instant relief. The sharp pain I had from my shoulder blade down my arm eased, allowing me to learn what a full night's sleep felt like again.

We got married a few months later, were getting settled and signing the dotted line on our new home, when everything changed and instead we packed our bags once again and jetted back off to London for a job opportunity to experience life on the other side of the world - the more grown up way. However, being far away with friends from home made a pretty fun setting for lots of laughs, parties, festivals, travels and more. We worked to pay for our good times, survived the 2008 global recession, travelled and continued on.

One weekend I landed back in the UK from a long-haul Sydney flight and thought it was a good idea to go to a party with jet lag. I stayed awake for far too many hours and my body finally said, "no more". It started with a migraine and quickly became shingles coming from the back of my neck up over my head down my forehead and in behind my left eye. It was so painful and awful it knocked me around. Even typing this now for you is making my head itch like crazy, isn't that weird? It was so severe I am still affected by bright lights and not able to see when there's the slightest glare.

My parents came to visit six months later and were stunned at what I was accepting to be a normal state. We lived above an underground tube line, in a tiny place in central London with our bedroom upstairs, so when they were with us they saw me lower myself down the stairs on my bottom using my hands and feet to move down slowly one step at a time.

The look on their faces was aghast: they had no idea I had been living like this. "It's not so bad," I said, "my body warms up after I have a shower and get some movement in my joints." However, I still needed assistance to put my stockings on, hold my toothbrush/hairbrush and do up my bra. Unscrewing bottle lids or holding saucepans when cooking were definitely not options.

Understandably, not wishing to see their child in pain and believing the cortisone injection was the fastest remedy to alleviate the pain, I was booked into the hospital and received an injection. Within 24 hours it was as though I had been put into a teenager's agile body. I could lift my knees to my chest and raise my arms above my head. I remember the absolute elation I felt and asked, "Is this what it's like to be a normal person?"

Wowee!

If it was, I wanted it and I wanted it all! I had no idea the pain I'd been putting up with and allowing myself to believe was just a normal part of my daily life. We went to Cornwall and had a wonderful family trip, we rambled up those cliffs with long walks, climbing down to beaches and up rock formations. It was a whole new lease of life!

I don't know how familiar you are with steroid injections but they vary depending on the person and the circumstances, and I was extremely fortunate mine was so successful. I was informed it would diminish within 1-2 months, but I hadn't realised it would be instantaneous. Disappearing as fast as it began, meaning within 24 hours you're back to what feels like a crippled state. I think it's worse on you mentally and emotionally. Ignorance was bliss previously, when I didn't know what I was missing. Added to that is the fact that in normal circumstances the pain increases gradually and builds over time, not BOOM and immediately being so debilitated you don't know what to do with yourself.

So I had another shot.

And another.

Until the doctors told me I'd had my quota for the year and it wasn't safe to have any more.

I was petrified. Suddenly knowing that state of having to rely on others to help me dress, open jars or carry heavy things was going to be my reality for the rest of my life was incredibly scary.

I was only 32 and still had hope of raising a family. How could I hold a baby if I could barely write with a pen?

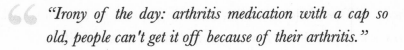

"Irony of the day: arthritis medication with a cap so old, people can't get it off because of their arthritis."

— KELLI JAE BAELI

The next couple of years brought huge amounts of change to my life.

Quite quickly I was introduced to a bodywork therapist, who also practised modern herbal medicine and lived around the corner from me, making house visits for massages twice a week achievable. I shifted to this form of treatment, taking herbs and continued to see the rheumatologist in parallel to cover all bases.

The problem was the doctor was advising me to take methotrexate, a disease modifying anti-inflammatory drug (DMARD), but the side effects for liver function, white blood cells, immunity suppressants and risk of causing birth defects were far too high to justify this, so I shunned the western medicine and focused solely on the holistic approach. I was advised this was risky and that I would pay the penalty in my later years, so I opted to continue blood tests and x-rays checking there were no joint disfigurations, whilst taking my herbal medicine and supplements.

From here the next few years of my life were unscripted. We moved house to Buckinghamshire seeking more space and green landscapes, suffered a miscarriage and a year later we were separating in preparation for divorce. We'd given it a go trying to fix things, but when you tape over a crack, it only works temporarily until the crack appears again. We had grown up since meeting at twenty and it became apparent we wanted different things for our future.

Do you know anyone that has gone through divorce? It's hard! I believe it's hard no matter what the circumstances. Children together or not. I was saying goodbye to someone I was once in love with and still loved. Our lives, our friends, our families were entwined.

Making the decision became the beginning of the end of a very significant chapter, which I made believing it was for the right reason, even though I had no idea what the future held.

The mere thought of change, especially with unknown circumstances ahead, can paralyse even the bravest amongst us. The loss of the familiar and an introduction to something new brings forth multiple mixed emotions. Fortunately though, change is often one of the best things that can happen in our lives.

It's a surreal experience and was emotionally draining. It took months of feeling lost afterwards, crying on the living room floor blaring Adele out of the stereo, before I was able to piece myself back together. He moved back to Australia, after our tearful goodbye, which was a blessing or we likely would've run back to each other's arms for that old "security blanket" familiar feeling.

> *"Self-awareness gives you the capacity to learn from your mistakes as well as your successes."*
>
> — *LAWRENCE BOSSIDY*

Months passed, I changed jobs and threw myself into my work. I had a great job with a luxury retail brand managing the southern Europe projects. Jackpot! I love to travel, explore new places, experience cultures and mingle with the locals, so getting paid to do it seemed perfect.

I can safely say this concerned my parents and as the saying goes, while they were happy for me to be happy, they also would've preferred for their little girl to come home after six years away. The tag line became "just don't fall in love with an Englishman!" They felt safer knowing I would return home when I was with my ex, but suddenly a new job, being single and free, who knew what was going to happen.

Then the inevitable did!

I met and fell in love with an Englishman [*insert the dramatic old movie sounds dun dun dunnnn*]. My whole world changed; he was different from anyone I had ever known. Older, originally from Yorkshire, opinionated, charming and incredibly sexy. I was different from anyone he'd known too - Australian, outgoing, cheeky, independent and streetwise.

Life inside our love bubble was perfect; sadly outside it was not so. There were external influences with a desire to make it as challenging for us as possible. Having lived through the difficulties of my own divorce, I didn't want to go through that again so packed my bags, left my (best) job and flew to the Seychelles to escape reality for a few months and dive into something I had always been passionate about as a hobby, but thought I was too old make a career change to - marine conservation.

I had three months in the Seychelles, snorkelling nearly every day identifying whale sharks, plus monitoring nesting turtles, and cleaning beaches and vegetation for turtle accessibility. Those tiny hatchlings are some of the cutest things I've ever seen. Their instinct to crawl out of the nest, along the sand straight for the beach is incredibly cool. Crabs, birds and dogs are predators for them (and that's before they even enter the big vast ocean) with only one in 1000 living to be an adult. So sad.

I loved this experience and it will live on within me forever. My broken heart intentions didn't quite go to plan (or maybe they did). Being on an island with strangers much younger can be incredibly lonely, so we were in touch regularly and he came to visit at the end of my tenure. He is possibly even more passionate than me about this wildlife, so all the while I was away he was incredibly envious. I took him to some of the best islands, and he saw his first turtles, tortoises, sharks and rays. We were in paradise and life was sweet. It all was superb until these huge cysts appeared on my leg, getting worse each day, multiplying and growing to the size of pus-filled bloody golf balls.

Eeeewww!

We stayed a few more days until it was up my left leg meridian line and we were advised to go straight to the hospital. I was able to see the head doctor for tropical diseases who proceeded to hack, squeeze and dig into my wounds without any anaesthetic every day for a week. Ouch! To save you the gory details, it was a flesh-eating bacteria that had entered my lymphatic system (lymphangitis) and I was lucky to be able to keep my left leg.

The real world and life's responsibilities were not on our side, so we quickly needed to depart this magical archipelago, flying in complete opposite directions for the UK and Australia. I was in fantastic hands for my medical treatment, however the recovery took many months, with the shock and impact on my body taking its toll. The scars today are still nasty looking bullet wounds.

Given what you know about shingles having an adverse effect on my autoimmune arthritis, I am sure you can imagine what this did too.

So my gallivanting around the world needed to cease. I was seeking treatment for all sorts, including fertility, only to find out that my tubes were blocked from the miscarriage I'd experienced six years earlier. It felt like one massive hurdle after another, with time not on my side and my lover on the other side of the world.

We hatched a plan to be back together again, which involved me moving back to the UK to allow him to continue a close loving relationship with his daughter. She was now thirteen years and still adjusting to her 'new normal' with her parents not being together so meeting me was challenging. We found ways to make it work. It was a new scenario for all of us, with many hurdles and obstacles, sprinkled with nice moments and learning to adapt to a new way of life too.

Throughout all of these years, I had been seeking treatment for what was an increasing list of health ailments. Some days were overwhelming and others manageable. I had continued on the holistic path with kinesiology, herbal tincture and supplements, combined with blood tests and x-rays to check my inflammation levels.

I found myself at a career fork in the road and was so perplexed what the best decision to make was that I sought the help of an energy healer a friend had mentioned. I received what I now fondly know as a life activation, a 22 strand DNA activation which awakens your divine blueprint, heightens your connection with your higher self, releases unconscious patterns, increases brain power, clears genetic karmic patterns, along with all of the excess clutter I had been trudging around with for years and years.

This was a life defining moment!

> "*You are searching the world for treasure, but the real treasure is Yourself.*"
>
> — *RUMI*

I'd love to be able to rewind, take character snapshots of who I was and how I thought prior to this and compare with who I am today.

I was seeking clarity, purpose and the ability to heal some of my life's wounds. I advanced to a new career and became more fascinated with this whole new world, which had been hiding in plain sight the whole time.

I received healing after healing, cutting emotional cords and relieving the lifetime load of baggage, until my Guide suggested I get certified to learn the tools to help heal myself.

A revelation.

I completed the initial course, received the certification and had an epiphany moment, where I realised there was more to it: it was bigger than me. Now I was able to help others similar to me, clueless there were options like this available to ease their pain too.

It cemented everything and I felt this new lease of life. The beauty of becoming an energy healer, or lightworker as we are also known, is that we get to heal ourselves along the way. During the training we learn, receive and give. I am continually evolving and healing along this path. It's a beautiful reciprocal synergy of life and the universe. The more light we provide and stand in, the more light is drawn into our being.

Incredible when you think about it.

You know the saying: when one door opens another closes. Instead I was finding five more doors opening. I was elated with the options of this brand new world and I wanted to learn so much more about it. I moved quickly on the Healers, Ritual Masters and Universal Kabbalah paths drawing in completely different universal energies, allowing me to delve into a deep journey to Know Thyself:

> "The closer you come to knowing that you alone create the world of your experience, the more vital it becomes for you to discover just who is doing the creating."

> — ERIC MICHA'EL LEVENTHAL

Self-awareness is the key.

The key to inner healing, self-love, self-worth, self-empowerment and remembering the knowledge we hold within.

My journey has been so transformational that I left my lifelong corporate career to build my own personal brand. Switching to something so brand new in my early 40s was daunting, but I knew I had to take the plunge. If I didn't I would always wonder what may have been.

It's been an exciting, challenging and rewarding rollercoaster journey shifting my mindset and finding my feet in the entrepreneurial world. I utilised an education platform to receive guidance, mentorship and accountability each step of the way, following in the footsteps of those that had walked before me, allowing me to now provide help to those seeking a sea change or more from their life.

> *"Our only limitation is what we believe is possible!"*
>
> — *ANON*

By spinning a few plates, I was able to organise our Italian wedding in parallel, with our loved ones joining us from across the world. There was talk of taking on too much, but I followed my heart and am grateful everything aligned for us to have the perfect day, especially now, one year later in 2020, knowing it would not have been possible.

Thank you, universe!

These last few years, my husband has witnessed my evolution and has now received multiple DNA activations himself, allowing him to progress alongside me on his journey at his own pace. He was incredibly grounded, traditional and set in his ways, so this process began to move him beyond his own limitations, helping us to find that halfway point between our approach in life.

It's been a growing experience for both of us.

Those close to me were hesitant about the direction I was heading, initially. Walking away from a long-standing successful career, to begin working within a new sector and the online space was a foreign concept. Perhaps I always knew it wasn't forever. I had interests elsewhere in property and marine conservation, but was unsure how to transition these beyond a hobby. In the end, my health and seeking more fulfilment is what brought alignment. I needed to fully trust myself to illustrate the benefits before they were visible.

The ripple effect now provides this automatically.

> *"It's impossible, said pride. It's risky, said experience. It's pointless, said reason. Give it a try, whispered the heart."*
>
> *— ANON*

For all of us, our healing is held within. Acknowledging this and leaning into more self-love has been an evolving process. I had to shed years of belittling thoughts, my old limiting beliefs and unworthiness, forming a new connection for self-love and self-worth to build fresh foundations within.

Life unfolds each day with twists and turns, ups and downs. I use the tools I have trained in to build my resilience for a brighter future, learning to respond to life, rather than react. It is incredibly personal, tough and rewarding, all bundled together requiring patience and self-love on multiple levels.

Rough days with inflammation and swelling still occur, but are fairly infrequent and generally linked to the heat or overindulgence. I now recognise the amber warning signs my body provides, realising it's time to surrender.

I have been prescription drug free for over a decade, utilising kinesiology, herbal medicine, energy healings, breathwork, electrolysed reduced water, cold therapy and a balanced lifestyle. I am physically active, with my main activities being walking, swimming, cycling and forms of body weight exercises. Anything outdoors in the sunshine too. Snorkelling is a favourite, but I also love walking through the woods or up a mountain, bringing satisfaction, happiness, endorphins and other high vibrations from within, linking me mentally, physically and emotionally.

I am now a "Conscious-Preneur" where lifestyle and business form one, the niche for creating a life you love, with sustainability, impact and soul led action. Focusing on yourself to go within, energise and rejuvenate yourself is praised, not a guilty pleasure.

The best part is, you can do it too! I would love to show you how. Follow your passion, learn new tools, build your brand and define your freedom lifestyle too.

"What do I want?" A simple question we rarely allow ourselves to ponder.

I can help you find your answer within.

We do not need to live in pain, nor allow our pain to define our future.

We magnetically attract a vibrational match into our lives. I choose to surround myself with inspiring individuals on similar trajectory paths, supporting each other's beliefs that more is possible.

And you can too!

"Never mind what is. Imagine it the way you want it to be so that your vibration is a match to your desire. When your vibration is a match to your desire, all things in your experience will gravitate to meet that match every time."

— *ABRAHAM HICKS*

ABOUT THE AUTHOR

MEGAN ROHAN TAYLOR

Meet Megan ...

Having endured days unable to dress herself or walk downstairs due to autoimmune and chronic disease, Megan knows only too well the difficulties one faces when our health is debilitated.

Following a lifelong corporate IT Project Management career, Megan embarked on a new venture to become a successful Holistic Healer and Online Business Lifestyle Mentor.

Living a holistic + healthy + conscious + thriving lifestyle.

When we heal, we are able to activate our blueprint within us to gain clarity for our life purpose.

After transitioning from her 25-year career, Megan built her own personal brand, opting to serve and help others create new opportunities for a 360 lifestyle approach for health, wealth and freedom.

Encompassing life and business approaches, people across the globe are empowered through a journey of self-discovery, soulful awakening and transformational alignment, allowing them to live with more fulfilment and purpose to create a life they love.

Megan founded Project Me - Uplevel Your Life FB Group, with a mission to fully support those that are seeking more from their life, creating a compelling vision, with empowering habits, energy alignment, stretch goals and soul-inspired potential to live their fullest life.

With an educational platform, community culture, personal growth and business opportunities, it means collaboration, masterminds, deeper connection and growth are possible, where we are able to create faster results with larger impact.

Megan's purpose and passion to inspire others will empower you to move towards your freedom lifestyle today too.

Magnetically attracting a vibrational match into our lives, Megan chooses to surround herself with inspiring individuals on similar trajectory paths, supporting each others' beliefs, with the knowledge that more is possible.

Would you like to join Megan to build your own online brand and create a life you love too?

Personal info

Hobbies : Travel, Photography, Scuba Diving, Marine Conservation, Nature & Holistic Health

Location : London, UK & Sydney, Australia

Contact

Email : meganrohantaylor@gmail.com
Web : www.meganrohantaylor.com
FB Group : https://www.facebook.com/
groups/ProjectMeUplevelYourLife/
Linktree : https://linktr.ee/mrohantaylor

instagram.com/meganrohantaylor

YOU DESERVE TO BE FULFILLED ON ALL LEVELS

"What's wrong, honey?" John asked with concern as he quickly pulled the car in at the side of the road. I was sobbing so hard that my whole body was shaking. He pulled me into his arms. "You can't continue like this," he said. "This is the second Christmas in a row that you are crying, and I know it's for the same reason as last year."

He was right, and I knew it. I was crying for the exact same reason I had the previous year and why I had been crying in solitude for the past few months. In so many ways, my life seemed perfect. We lived on a gorgeous little finca in the south of Spain. I was teaching yoga at a stunning studio overlooking a golf course, close to where we lived. I adored my job. I felt so lucky and proud that I got to do this for a living. My classes were doing well. I had a growing community of dedicated yoga students. 2017 had been an incredibly exciting year for personal and professional growth. I felt deeply fulfilled on so many levels, apart from one crucial one – financially, despite doing what I loved for a living, I was unable to support myself and it was crushing me.

MY YOGA JOURNEY

My journey to yoga was a simple one. Love at first step on the mat. Coming from the world of competitive gymnastics in my teens and becoming a young professional in my 20s, yoga was a natural and very welcome antidote to the stresses of corporate life and quickly became an essential part of my daily routine.

Working as a financial accountant in Dublin and deeply unsatisfied in my career, I longed for the kind of life where I could spend a larger part of my mornings practising yoga and meditation. Time was such a precious commodity and having a ritual like that seemed like an unattainable luxury, especially as each morning I would have to rush out the door at 7.15am to catch the bus to the city centre where I worked.

My job was stressful to say the least, but my short morning routine kept me sane and a little better equipped to manage myself and life. I hated the commute, though, and I hated my job. It felt so far removed from what I really wanted for my life and in 2009 I started to dream about what it would be like to become a yoga teacher. What it would be like to have more time in my day to practise the things I loved; to work in an environment that wasn't stressful and with people who enjoyed what they did and were happy to be there.

My gratitude journal started to fill with anticipation of all the things I wanted to manifest in my life. I started to paint the pictures and give thanks for the things that were to come.

Around the same time, I started to delve into online trading and slowly began to build a business around this. I started to get up even earlier to do my 'extra' work, but I always made time for my yoga practice before anything else.

I BELIEVE IN DESTINY!

By 2012, I had made the switch to full time trading online, and John and I felt strongly that we wanted to leave Dublin. We were tired of city life and had a strong desire to spend more time doing the things we loved and were passionate about (aka yoga and kitesurfing).

It was a Sunday in July and pouring with rain (again) in Dublin. "What about Spain?" I said to John.

His eyes lit up straight away. "It would certainly be better than here," he said laughing as he looked out the window.

"Do you think you could get a transfer with work?" I asked.

"I can certainly ask!" he said.

The following day John approached his manager. "I might have something for you," he said to John's surprise. And just two days later we received a phone call to confirm he would start in Alicante, Spain, in four weeks' time.

I believe in destiny and my experience has been that when things move fast they are meant to be.

As promised, four weeks later, John started work in Alicante airport. And six weeks after that, with everything finalised, rented or sold in Ireland, we were fully settled in our new home in Spain, a lovely house overlooking the sea and right next to a natural park. Honestly, we could hardly believe our luck.

We effortlessly slipped into Spanish life and my morning rituals continued much the same as back in Dublin, albeit the view from my yoga mat was far nicer and the weather, far better. My walks with the doggies became adventure filled hikes in the natural park close to our new home. It was bliss!

My career as a trader, even though it provided me with geographical freedom, was even more stressful than my job as a corporate accountant, and the idea of becoming a yoga teacher still danced away in the back of my mind!

"How amazing would it be to teach yoga in this stunning place?" I thought to myself.

After a couple of years, we knew we wanted to buy a permanent home in Alicante and, unable to find anything in the immediate area, we cast our net a little wider. Doing this allowed us to look at some larger properties and fincas (the Spanish term for farmhouse). Not long into our search, John fell hard for a small finca on 3800 sq. metres with lemon and orange groves and a house consisting of eight bedrooms, a guest house and a pool. All for roughly the same price as our three-bed semi in Dublin.

To be honest, I wasn't as keen on the house as John, but I could see the immense potential it had as a possible yoga retreat. It had buckets of space, was surrounded by natural woodland (ideal for long walks) and it was a five-minute drive to the beach. It seemed perfect, and with my trading business floundering it seemed like the perfect next step for my career.

As soon as our offer was accepted on the house, I knew my time had finally come to train as a yoga teacher. The dream I had had since 2009 was about to become a reality.

As I mentioned before, I believe when things happen fast, they are meant to be. I found a 200-hour intensive yoga teacher training not far from where we lived. And two weeks later, with John's blessing and a mixture of trepidation and excitement, off I went for three very intense but incredible weeks of training, learning and practising. It was the most extraordinary experience and I definitely returned home a completely changed woman.

As soon as we moved into our new home, I found a yoga studio close by to practise at myself, and not long after, the studio owner asked if I wanted to teach there. I was ecstatic. I couldn't believe my luck, just out of yoga school and I landed an actual teaching job! I was beside myself!

From the beginning, I loved teaching yoga. It brought me so much joy and energy. My classes were really tiny to begin. I was lucky to have two or three people join me initially, but I felt so grateful for each and every one. And even though I made an absolute pittance for my time, I didn't care because I was so happy to be doing something that I truly loved and that lit me up inside!

After some months living in our new home, I realised the immense task of setting up a retreat centre and didn't think I was quite ready for that, but I was still determined to teach yoga from there. We converted the open plan living room in our house, laying down wooden floors and equipping the space with mats, blankets, blocks and bolsters. In September 2015, I opened my small studio which I called NivaYoga (Niva is a play on my name that means 'the Sun' in Sanskrit but also means to restore, revive, replenish and renew http://nivayoga. mystrikingly.com/) where I offered classes and workshops and with the help of word of mouth and Facebook community pages, I started to build a small group of regular students.

I had to keep the cost of the classes low to be competitive or at least comparable to other local studios, but as my little studio was in our home I had no major overheads, so all income came directly to me and this made it somewhat justifiable.

I really wasn't making much money at all, though, and while I felt blessed that John had a good job, it was starting to irritate me that I couldn't afford to contribute more to our household expenses. I had always been super independent. I had always earned my own money even as a teenager; I always had a job. And from University I went into a highly paid professional career, so it pained me that I couldn't afford to contribute more to our household and worse still, I had to depend on John.

Further to that, I desperately wanted to attend another teacher training to deepen my knowledge but that was a complete no-no, as what little money I did earn went towards the bills. The only solution I could think of to make more money was to teach more classes, which I knew I needed to do but I had no car because, well, I couldn't afford that either.

Amid my frustration, a few things kept coming up:

Firstly, in yoga, we are taught to have 'non-attachment'. I was taught that I shouldn't be 'attached' to the concept of money, and that by having 'attachment' and wanting more for myself I wasn't being 'spiritual' or 'yogic'. The idea of the renunciate Yogis of ancient India weighed heavily on my mind. Who was I to want more? Was I just a stupid 'wannabe' yogi from the west? Should I renounce all my desires for my life in order to be more 'yogic'?

This pained me deeply and left me feeling conflicted, because on one hand I wanted to be a devout yogini and teacher, but on the other hand I had spent years cultivating a mindset around the law of attraction and trusted deeply that I could have and create whatever I wanted for my life. But now, on my yoga journey, I felt I ought to renounce my personal beliefs as well as all material wealth and abundance, which just didn't feel right to me.

Secondly, I adored teaching yoga and treasured the idea of doing what I loved for a living. I wanted so much to trust that the Universe would bring me just rewards for doing what I love and bringing joy to others. But I felt that I was being forced to undercharge to be comparable/competitive with other studios and I felt hurt that my time, effort, energy and passion were not being rewarded as I felt they should.

Thirdly, one of my best friends worked in marketing and she encouraged me to post more on social media. "You need to be present on social media every day so that people know you exist," she said. It made sense to me as a way to grow my business but the idea of sharing my life on social media made me feel icky and un-yogic. "Who would be interested in that anyway?" I thought. "No, thank you. I'll just rely on the good grace of the Universe to help me."

Luckily, interest in my classes did start to grow somewhat through word of mouth and with that I knew I wanted to teach more, to train more and that I desperately needed to make more money. Further to that, running a business from our home was starting to take its toll on our home life and it became clear that in order to grow my business, I needed to move out of my little studio and go in search of somewhere new, somewhere bigger and more central where there were more people, rather than being hidden away in the countryside where we were hard to find. (Had I known how to market myself correctly this would never have been an issue.)

At that time, I was personally taking classes with a wonderful teacher who had arrived in Alicante from London the previous year. She was highly experienced, having spent fifteen years running two high profile studios in London, and I was blown away by her knowledge and knew from the first class I attended with her that I wanted her to be my next teacher.

The studio where she was teaching was amazing, so perfect and exactly what I had had in mind for myself. I thought to myself, "Perhaps if I can convince Helena to mentor me then maybe with a little luck perhaps I could come teach some classes at her studio too." I finally picked up the courage to ask her and to my sheer joy she agreed.

The training we did spanned over eight weeks and was mind blowing. It was everything I wanted from a training and more and my confidence as a teacher grew exponentially. I was still on the hunt for a new studio and having not found anything yet, every time I went to the studio, I kept thinking "I would just love to teach here" and I would visualise myself doing so which was easy because we had done our training there. I kept secretly hoping Helena would ask me to come teach there with her.

It was a Sunday morning at the beginning of December 2016 when my prayers (and visualisations) were answered and Helena asked me if I could take over the Sunday morning class from January. I jumped at the chance; it was finally happening! I knew my patience and persistence had paid off.

Attendance at my own classes slowed considerably in the run up to Christmas and I was feeling really anxious about the lack of money I had coming up to our biggest annual holiday. The pressure of it weighed down on me like a tonne of bricks. I had saved as much as I could during the previous months, but I knew it wasn't going to be enough. I knew I was going to have to ask John to help me out and I hated that.

A few days before Christmas, John and I drove to the local city to do some shopping. We had some presents to get and John wanted to buy some new clothes. John selected a few things for himself and went to the fitting room to try them on.

As I waited for him, the lady's section of the shop caught my eye and I went to take a look. I've always loved shopping for myself and had done so frivolously throughout my previous corporate careers. I excitedly scanned the rail and I pulled out a gorgeous pair of jeans and, not thinking, I ran to the changing room and tried them on. They were so nice, and they fit like a glove. I looked at the price tag - €40. I stopped for a moment and my breath caught as my heart sank and I knew I couldn't buy them. I just didn't have enough money and I couldn't ask John for more help.

I was both devastated and mortified. How had it come to this? I was thirty-five years old, highly educated, doing a job that I adored and that fulfilled me on so many levels, but I couldn't afford to buy myself a pair of jeans. This was not how my life was supposed to be! I was so upset I cried the whole way home in the car, to John's bewilderment.

I GOT THE CALL

Just after New Year's in January 2017 I got a call from Helena. She had had a family emergency and needed to leave Alicante ASAP and asked if I would be able to take over her classes at the studio.

Despite being desperately sad to lose her as a mentor and friend, my heart leapt for joy! "This was meant for you!" said John's mum, who was with me when the call came through. I knew she was right. This felt like the best present I had ever received, and an absolute dream come true. The excitement was unreal!

Without doubt, 2017 was to be my greatest year yet as a yoga teacher. I was the lead teacher at my dream studio and the popularity of my classes didn't just grow but truly went from strength to strength.

Helena's motto had been that "yoga should be affordable for everyone" and according to her, we should encourage people to come to practise as often as possible by keeping our prices really low so that people could afford it, citing that the 'low price' would stimulate further growth in our yoga community.

Her theory made complete sense to me conceptually but deep down it felt wrong. However, as I was in a place of immense gratitude toward her, and keen to continue the good work that she had started, and knew her ideas echoed the yogic philosophy of 'non-attachment', I maintained the prices at the levels she had established which were €5 to drop in and €40 for a 10x class ticket.

This was already a great deal lower than what I had been charging for classes in my home studio and I would have to attract consistently high numbers of students to support myself. On top of that, I now had to pay the studio owner forty percent of the class takings. I also had additional costs. I had to buy a car (yikes) and insure, tax and fuel it. I had to travel to and from the studio, taking more time out of my day (one class took roughly four to five hours). Ultimately, what this meant was, I had to work harder than ever to make sure class numbers stayed strong, teach more classes and workshops and think of any other ways I could to make money.

Again, I felt conflicted. "You're doing what you love, Niamh. This is what you wanted!" I would tell myself. "Just get on with it and do what you have to do!"

I started to plan. I was teaching six days per week. My yoga classes were going great: I was averaging really good numbers. I started to teach a monthly workshop on Saturdays that sold out most months and was a great bonus for me. I started to teach some English as well to help me financially because I just couldn't physically teach more yoga.

As summer approached, I was very aware that class numbers would drop back with the season. I knew I needed to offer something beyond the classes, so I decided to hold a retreat. I had always wanted to share my morning rituals, so this seemed like an ideal opportunity to do so and I created a four-day mini morning rituals retreat, which was a great success.

I found it extremely difficult to set the price of the retreat as I could just hear Helena's voice telling me to 'make it affordable'! As it was my first retreat and I felt inexperienced, I priced the whole weekend at €45 per person for meditation, yoga and breakfast (which I prepared myself) for four days.

When I think of it now, I shudder, and can only recall my best friend's horrified face when I told her how little I was charging. Despite the retreat selling out and being a huge success, I barely covered my costs and felt drained in every way afterwards.

I really wanted to be able to take some time off but felt a huge obligation to my students who had become like family, and I didn't want to let them down by taking time off even though I was exhausted! As I mentioned above, every class took around four to five hours out of my day and along with the English classes I was teaching and working six days per week, I was pooped!

As well as feeling like I didn't want to let my students down, I also knew that no teaching meant no income, so I felt very reluctant to take any time for myself. However, I knew I needed to and the best possible solution I could come up with was to get someone to cover when I needed time off. So I put the feelers out and one of my regular students was keen to do it. She was completing her 200-hour training but as I wanted to maintain a standard and style in the studio, we agreed to teach her the same style of programme that Helena had taught me. The training I had received was invaluable and I was keen to pass it on, as I knew it would instil the confidence in her to be a strong, highly supportive and knowledgeable teacher. And who doesn't want that?

We agreed to do a 100-hour training over six weeks but due to feeling inexperienced in myself and again that voice in my head that said, 'keep it affordable', I only charged €300 for my time and knowledge. "It's an amazing experience and opportunity so just be grateful!" I told myself, but deep down I knew this was way too low a price and it gave me a sinking feeling in the pit of my stomach. On top of that, I had to give up my one free day per week to do this training. So, I was teaching seven days per week.

I FINALLY GOT TO TRAIN!

Furthering my education has always been top of my agenda and throughout the year, I had been planning to attend a Yin Yoga Teacher training with a teacher I had been following for a few years by that stage. I had made contact about the training centre earlier in the year and was told there were places available, but I didn't have any money at the time to pay for it so I had to wait.

By August, though, having made extra money from my retreat and from my teacher training, I finally had enough money saved (Yay!), so I got in touch to book the course only to be told it was completely SOLD OUT! I was devastated. I had been working so hard to save and I missed it. I actually started to cry as I had been telling people how excited I had been about the course and I couldn't wait to attend.

When I came to terms with the fact it wasn't going to happen, I had a look online and there happened to be a different Yin Training happening in Spain around that same week as the training I had wanted to attend. I didn't know the teacher, but I thought to myself, "I'll just do it and get the certificate, and anyway it will be cheaper for me as I don't have to travel too far, so bonus, right?"

Wrong!

I attended the training in late October and from the outset, I didn't get on that well with the trainer. We just seemed to clash from day one. I had been teaching Yin Yoga for a couple of years by this time and had been studying it intensively at home and online. I was deeply passionate about the practice and my classes were popular. We had on occasion had to turn people away as we had run out of space. It wasn't clear when this teacher trainer had last taught a public class of Yin Yoga and her way of teaching which she made us practise felt really unnatural and wrong for me. I really struggled. Further to that, the level of the anatomy being taught wasn't quite as high as I would have expected, and I felt I knew more than what she was teaching. Overall, I felt deeply saddened, frustrated and quite honestly angry.

"How could I have been so stupid?" I berated myself. I had been saving all year for this training. I had worked so incredibly hard to get the money. I was completely exhausted and close to burnout and now the training which I had spent my hard-earned money on felt like an absolute waste of time. "I should have known better than to attend a training with a teacher I don't know," I thought as the tears rolled down my face.

Returning home, I found it really difficult to settle back into my class timetable. I felt disjointed. I felt uneasy in my teaching, and my passion-driven energy was gone.

With Christmas fast approaching, the class numbers dwindled as they do at that time of year. John and I set out for our usual outing to the city to do some Christmas shopping. John went to try some things on and I had a look around only to spot a really nice pair of jeans! I looked at them. "Oh, they're lovely," I thought to myself and I looked at the tag… "€39.99"…. My eyes welled up. My family was arriving in a couple of days and I needed to buy presents and other things. "I can't afford them."

As we finished up our shopping and went back to the car, I couldn't control the tears. They began to flow like water. "What's wrong, honey?" John asked with concern as he quickly pulled the car in at the side of the road. By now, I was sobbing so hard that my whole body was shaking so he pulled me into his arms. "You can't continue like this. It's the second Christmas in a row that you are crying, and

I know it's for the same reason as last year." He was right. I was crying for the exact same reason I had the previous year and why I had been crying in solitude the past few months.

"I would have bought those jeans for you, you know," said John. I sobbed harder. I knew he would have but I didn't want him to because I wanted to be able to buy those jeans for myself. I wanted to be able to fully support myself and be able to buy the things I needed when I needed them.

In so many ways, my life seemed perfect. We lived in the south of Spain. I was teaching yoga at a stunning studio. I adored my job. I felt so lucky and proud and without doubt 2017 had been an incredibly exciting year for me professionally. I had achieved so many things. I felt deeply fulfilled on so many levels apart from one crucial one – financial.

Looking back now, I know a huge part of my problem was due to an unsupportive inherited money mindset, but at that time I felt like a complete failure. Despite doing what I loved, I was exhausted, burnt out and flat broke. I knew something drastic had to change and that my life couldn't continue this way, but I also knew there had to be another way, a better way to do this and I was determined to find it!

CHANGE IS IN THE AIR...

By mid-January 2018, I was already setting the wheels of change in motion. Firstly, I sat down and got completely clear on all the things I wanted for my life. I knew I wanted to be happy, successful, thriving and completely fulfilled in ALL areas of my life and work. I wanted to be paid well for the work that I do. I wanted to be able to take holidays or sick days and know that I am taken care of. I wanted to have time for myself, to nourish myself and take yoga classes for myself. I wanted to be able to afford to travel, to go on retreat and to attend yoga teacher trainings when I wished. I wanted to be fulfilled on all levels, physically, emotionally, spiritually and financially and I didn't want to feel guilty for that. I also truly wanted to be able to fill my cup and operate and teach from this well of fullness. And most of all, I wanted to figure out how to create a sustainable yoga business model that supports its biggest asset, the teacher.

I had no idea how I was going to do this, but I was intent on making this my mission. What I did know was that I needed to make some money to figure this out and the only realistic way I knew how to do that quickly was to return to my corporate job as an accountant. Going back to corporate life was my absolute worst nightmare but I was determined to do whatever it took to figure out how to create the life I had been dreaming of and to feel fulfilled on all levels.

As I mentioned, I believe in destiny and I also believe that when you set a path in motion, get very clear on what it is you want to create, and set clear intentions out to the Universe, then pathways magically open up in the most unexpected places.

LOOKING FOR SOLUTIONS

Even though I hadn't worked as an accountant in eight years, I magically managed to get a job in an insurance company in Gibraltar which was six hours' drive from where we lived in Alicante. Returning to Ireland had been the obvious choice for this change but it just didn't feel right to me, yet Gibraltar, despite not knowing anyone there, felt really right!

And like so many things in my life before that point, once the plan was in place and the intentions clear, everything I needed to make the changes showed up right on cue and within roughly eight weeks I was established in a new life, new career, large salary and on the road to making my dreams a reality.

With my bank account being replenished I took time to fill my cup. I started to practise for myself again at a fantastic studio I found, where I was also invited to come teach. I travelled to Goa, India to a yoga retreat. I took two trainings with the Yin Yoga trainer I had initially wanted to train with, one in Germany and one in Switzerland. Life was pretty good, and I knew it would have been easy for me to continue this way, but I couldn't forget the mission I had set for myself.

While still in Zurich, Switzerland, at the second Yin Yoga training, I felt the deep urge to get started on my mission and so from my little Air BnB, I began searching around on YouTube for possible solutions. To be honest, I didn't really know what I was looking for when an ad popped up with a guy called Emil, offering a free workshop series to explain how to build an online business around your passions.

I initially went to stop the ad because I've always been sceptical of these things, but he seemed like such a nice, ordinary guy and what he was saying really resonated with me, so I kept listening. He spoke about the idea of working with things that you are truly passionate about (like yoga) which was really interesting. "What do I have to lose?" I thought as I signed up for the free workshops.

As I delved into the workshops which were given by Emil's personal online business mentor, Stuart, I was still sceptical as I knew it was going to be some kind of sales pitch but to be honest I was really intrigued by what he was discussing. He spoke in detail about two online business models (affiliate marketing and e-commerce) which once set up could create passive income. This seemed like the perfect solution. If I could create passive income for myself, I could return to teaching yoga full time and not have to worry about taking holidays or sick days; I would be covered during seasonal downturns; there would always be some income coming in.

He went on to explain that it takes work to set it up initially but once up and running then it keeps working for you around the clock. "Well, I am certainly no stranger to hard work," I thought, "and if it gets me closer to my goal then it will be worth it. Plus, maybe learning the digital marketing side could help me to grow my yoga business too!"

The sceptic in me was screaming, "Scam, Scam," but something inside was telling me to pay attention. Creating passive income of any kind always seemed to be a thing of myths. After all, online trading was sold to me as a way to create 'passive income' but it turned out to be anything but passive. However, this affiliate marketing and e-commerce seemed plausible. "I could sell yoga mats, blocks, leggings, etc." I thought.

I have always believed anything is possible with a little hard work. And I was determined to figure out how to create a sustainable yoga business for myself, so I signed up for the first basic course and I began my journey into this brand-new world of digital marketing.

I dove straight into the first part of the training whilst still in Zurich and totally loved it. It was fascinating, and I ended up getting through it quite quickly. Hungry for more, I upgraded to the next level training and then the next, and the next. I also signed up for another course on creating online courses, workshops and masterminds.

I hoovered up the knowledge, loving every minute and completely immersed myself in the community which was filled with like-minded individuals, all looking to create a life of true fulfilment. Something very surprising to me was that our community of digital entrepreneurs ('The Tribe' as it's known) has a deeply spiritual undertone. This was not something I was expecting at all. And when, on my first coaching session with my Elite mentor, she pulled out a pack of angel cards to start our conversation, I knew I was at home!

It didn't take me long to find my own 'tribe' and develop deep personal relationships of mutual support and growth. We were learning so much more than to build an online business from scratch and become experts in digital marketing, a skill set which is absolutely essential for every business across the globe today. We were learning how to authentically reach people. How to connect with them on a deeper level. How to create meaningful impact in the world while blossoming into your true self, sharing your unique message and becoming the person you were born to be.

THE RESULT

My business now consists of a growing high-ticket affiliate marketing business, two online courses born out of my natural superpowers and a third in the pipeline, available for purchase online. Both the affiliate marketing business and the courses are generating monthly passive income for my business. I also do freelance work with an amazing company that I am so proud to be part of using the digital skills I have acquired; my proud title is "Find Your Purpose Mentor and Email Marketing Specialist". Further to this, I have income from the yoga classes I now teach online per week and for which I now charge accordingly because I value my worth. Ultimately, I have created what I set out to create - A SUSTAINABLE YOGA BUSINESS MODEL that supports its greatest asset, the teacher.

My digital journey has taught me many things, but the following have been the most astonishing:

1. I had inherited crippling limiting beliefs around money and what I could charge as a yoga teacher.
2. My intense lack of self-worth had prevented me charging accordingly or putting myself and my gifts out there in an effective way.
3. I lacked the marketing knowledge and understanding necessary to effectively run a business and now believe this should be an essential module in all yoga teacher trainings.
4. The yoga business is a real business and should be treated as such.
5. Selling/marketing is not icky or un-yogic. You

have gifts and talents to share with the world so go do that with pride.

6. Technology isn't scary and is an enormous asset when you take the time to learn.

7. Yoga teachers do amazing work and deserve to live a life that is fulfilled on all levels.

I know I am not the only yoga teacher out there who has experienced intense struggles in her yoga business.

I know there are so many devoted teachers out there who are truly passionate about sharing their knowledge and making a positive impact on the lives of others; but who, just like me, are barely surviving by teaching classes alone and really struggling to know their worth.

Teachers who feel the intense pressure to keep their class prices low or give free classes, completely undervaluing themselves and their gifts.

Teachers who are exhausted or worse still, burnt out, from the current yoga business model, where the only realistic way they know to increase their income is to teach more classes.

Teachers who don't know how to effectively promote their beautiful offerings as this is not taught in yoga teacher training and being on social media feels icky and 'un-yogic'.

Teachers who were petrified that they would have to give up their dream and return to their previous corporate career as they failed to support themselves from their passion.

Teachers who have come too far to give up now and know there must be a better way but just don't know what that better way is!

I know I have found the 'better way' and it involves a massive mindset shift and creating passive income through going digital.

With the onset of Covid-19 and the intense dash for yoga teachers everywhere to shift their business online, a whole host of additional difficulties have arisen. I feel that the shift to a sustainable yoga business model is needed more than ever.

From my desire to share what I have learned on my journey, 'The Digital Yogini' (www.thedigitalyogini.com) has been born. Through 'The Digital Yogini' I want to empower yoga teachers who are struggling, like I was, to truly harness the tools and resources available to them so they can make the shift from surviving to thriving and create the life they have been dreaming of.

I see 'The Digital Yogini' as much more than just a brand name. I see her as the yoga teacher who refused to settle for a life that was not fulfilled on all levels but chose to love herself enough to reclaim her self-worth, and value herself at the highest levels so that she could be the person she was born to be and create the impact she is truly here to make.

If she is YOU, please know that you are not alone. I've got you!

And if you are not a yoga teacher, I hope my story will inspire you to truly value your worth and never give up on creating the life you have been dreaming of.

Sending you all my love,

Namaste,

Niamh x

ABOUT THE AUTHOR

NIAMH ASPLE

Niamh is a dedicated yogini, yoga teacher, soulpreneur and mentor.

Having struggled to survive by teaching yoga classes alone, and finding herself burnt out and broke following the conventional yoga business model, she set out to find a way to create a more sustainable yoga business model that supports its greatest asset, the teacher.

Niamh now empowers yoga teachers to harness all the tools and resources available to them to grow their yoga business in a way that meets their needs and make the shift from surviving to thriving.

Niamh's biggest hope with writing this chapter is that all readers will be inspired to value themselves at the highest level and not settle with something just because they are being led to believe it is the right way.

It's her firm belief that you deserve to live a life that is fulfilled on all levels and her biggest wish is that you get out there and truly create the life you have been dreaming of.

She is dedicating her chapter to her amazing husband, John, whose support has been unwavering throughout her journey. Without him she is not sure if she would have survived the low points, but his encouragement has helped her to not only not give up but to find a better way.

Contact:

Website: https://thedigitalyogini.com
Email: niamh@thedigitalyogini.com
Facebook: www.facebook.com/thedigitalyogini

facebook.com/nianh.asple.3
instagram.com/thedigitalyogini

SARAH BOULTER

*W*hen I was offered the opportunity to be part of this collaboration book someone else nearly said no.

Someone else nearly let fear get the better of her, told herself to come back down to earth, that no one would be interested in her story and that she'd just make a fool of herself.

That someone else was the old me. A girl crippled by low self-esteem and limiting beliefs. Somebody who often let her thoughts and actions be shaped by a fear of the opinions of others. Someone who just simply never thought she was good enough.

So I almost didn't make it here, but then the hero of the story stepped up (you'll like her; she's pretty cool). The new me who's learned that if I'm bold, if I say yes now and then work out the how later, if I feel the fear and do it anyway, then wonderful things happen.

So, she said yes, and now here I am, ready to proudly share my story for the first time. Excited that it might inspire just one other person to know that they have absolutely everything they need within them right now to live the life they were made for.

And right now, I am creating the life of my dreams, the one I know is meant for me. I am building a six-figure business around being a full-time mum to my two beautiful boys. I have endless possibilities in front of me and feel confident to take any path I choose because I believe that I can do anything I want to.

It sounds wonderful, doesn't it? It is!

But life wasn't always this way because I wasn't always this way. It's been a long journey which at times has been incredibly painful with some extremely hopeless low points. I've had a moment which I can remember as vividly as if it were yesterday when I sat in the bath and decided there was just no point to life any more. At that time, I truly decided I had nothing to give and was nothing but a burden, that everyone I loved would be better off without me around. That dark moment was part of a long battle with anxiety and depression that had been hiding under an eating disorder as its outlet for fifteen years, but it was also a pivotal turning point.

They say when you reach rock bottom then the only way is up, and I believe this wholeheartedly. Some of the most significant achievements in our lives can come after reaching a point of no return. This is often when we have no choice but to delve deep and make huge change. What I've learnt over the years, though, is that you don't have to wait for rock bottom. There are signs around us all the time that are trying to show us an opportunity to move in alignment to who and where we should be.

The trouble is that often the signs get seen, the excitement inside us sparks but then very quickly something else creeps in. It has many disguises and takes multiple forms – excuses, procrastination, limiting beliefs, negative self-talk - but under them all is one thing: fear.

It's a sneaky little beast, fear, because it confuses you and it's easy to fall for its tricks. With the unpleasant physical sensations that accompany fear you'd be forgiven for caving in and thinking, "Clearly I'm meant to turn around and run the other way!" and if you need any further evidence then fear will call in the help of one of its side-kicks and get limiting belief to talk you out of anything exciting you might be about to consider. But there is one thing that fear simply can't get past. Something that can stop it in its path and put it back where it belongs every time. You see, there is only one thing we need to be able to make decisions that create the life we were destined for. It's something that each and every one of us has already built inside us – courage.

It sounds easy, doesn't it? Have courage, conquer fear and take on the world. If it was that simple then no one would get stuck. We'd all be living our best life, sharing our joy, bearing our light and speaking our truth like we are meant to. But finding your courage and learning to use it all the time, every day – to make being courageous a habit – isn't easy because fear is strong and limiting beliefs are deep rooted. We can't always get past those on our own, especially if we've allowed them to remain present and gain strength for a long time.

There are so many things we can do to help ourselves when we find ourselves suppressed and struggling. I've done them all at some point and believe each has massive value – counselling, journalling, self-help books and videos, they've all played a part in my journey but at forty years old I can tell you the biggest thing I've learnt which is summed up beautifully in this quote:

> *"We already have the answers within us. We always have had. We're already enough. We always have been. We just learned to forget."*
>
> — *RUMI*

And we do forget. Life experiences can shape us in ways we didn't expect, send us down a different path and influence the person we become. Before we know it, we are lost along the way, but we learn to accept, to be grateful for what we have and to settle. Now, please understand I'm a huge advocate of gratitude and I practise it every day. There is nothing wrong with being happy with what you have, but if you had big dreams, if there is something unfulfilled inside you, if your purpose is still not found, your gift still not shared, then that will continue to eat at you – it's trying to tell you something.

If you've picked up this book, then you're probably not a "settler" and you are probably seeking something. So let me share my story because realising your potential and fulfilling your destiny IS meant for you and often all we need is some inspiration and a bit of girl power to help light up that fire that's already inside you and bring out that courage to make your move.

Like most of you I've always had this feeling I was meant for more – something pretty big actually. Even though I wasn't sure exactly what it was, the feeling was always there. The feeling that there was more to life and so much more to me. That I wanted to serve people by sharing something special – again, I didn't know what that was, it was just a burning desire in the form of a dream.

Those dreams start when we are children. We dream without fear and we dream big – we truly believe we can be anything we want to be when we grow up. (I wanted to be everything from a vet, to an air hostess, to a painter and decorator!)

Nothing seems impossible when we are young. Then life starts to happen, we learn the word No – we hear it a lot! We get put into classes and tested on our abilities; we get graded and labelled. We get judged on our appearance, our intellect, our monetary status and our beliefs – sometimes that's positive and sometimes it isn't. Gradually life experiences and the opinions of others start to shape our thoughts, limit our beliefs and shrink those dreams. And often caught up in there can be the voice that has something to say and the gift that we must share.

But that voice and that gift (our purpose) is that constant pull we can feel, that burning desire that even when suppressed just will not go away. It's only my opinion formed on personal experience but I truly believe that a big cause of anxiety and depression in some people is that unmet need, that unspoken story, that unshared gift, that stunted creativity that is meant to be out in the world. For me this quote explains that beautifully:

> *"The definition of hell is meeting the person you could have become."*
>
> — DAVE ULLOA

Like so many of you reading this book, over the years I have let limiting beliefs shape more of me than I should have. I fell into thinking that success, wealth and true happiness (the kind where you light up inside because everything is in alignment) was reserved for others. And as I mentioned earlier I regularly did that thing that we do (especially us ladies) where we justify staying stuck and feeling unfulfilled because we know we should be grateful for what we have, because we are so much better off than lots of others. For the parents amongst us there is an even better one - almost undeniable in fact, that we've had our chance and now our children should come first; they will get the chances we didn't have.

And whilst that may be true, so is this – you owe it to yourself, your children and the rest of the world to live your life to the fullest as the best version of you, letting out everything that's in there that will serve, inspire and empower others.

If you really are better off than a lot of others, then does that not mean you're in a better position to inspire? If you are lucky enough to have a nice comfortable life then will that not make it easier for you start something, speak up, create, lead the way? And if you're not, then doesn't that simply mean you have nothing to lose and absolutely everything to gain by creating massive change?

And for the parents, yes, absolutely our children come first, their needs must be met and making them feel safe and loved is paramount, but please recognise you have the potential to influence, inspire and empower your children more than anyone else. You have the ability to cancel out lots of those limiting beliefs before they even start to form by demonstrating the opposite. If you really want your children to live a life of their dreams where anything is possible, are you showing them how that's done? Do they see you with a sense of purpose doing something that lights you up from the inside? Can they see that you are proud of yourself and your achievements?

Don't let your children be your excuse not to pursue your potential. Instead make them your reason to.

I think it is safe to say that if you've picked up a book entitled "There She Glows" then you are looking to be inspired and empowered. So let's do exactly that, because my aim here is to leave you knowing two things for certain. Firstly, that every one of us has the choice to make change at any given moment; it's all in our hands. And secondly, you already have what you need to do that within you, you really do, we often just forget how powerful we are and how much we have already been capable of.

One thing that's helped me greatly in my journey to success is to reflect back on all the times I've been bold and courageous in the past, because actually it's something I've always possessed – that feisty fighting spirit has always been there. It's a very simple exercise but if you simply take the time to timeline and journal any decisions you've made or changes you've incorporated, you'll start to realise what a bad ass you already are! Don't forget to include the little stuff because even seemingly small decisions can take a lot of courage to execute at times.

I have said already that all we really need is courage and that we all possess that inside, but learning how to use it often and almost habitually is the key to saying yes to opportunity and to striving forward to create a life of your dreams, whatever that may look like for you. Reminding yourself how brave you already are and what you've overcome to get this far will allow you to empower yourself.

Sometimes it's easier to hear someone else's story first to help you realise how powerful the simple things are. And that's exactly what my story is, very simple. There is nothing special about me and I wouldn't say I've overcome anything particularly out of the ordinary, but to me they were big things and they led me to where I am now, because reflecting back on the past allowed me to remember who I am – and change the game.

Back when I was seventeen, I was at that very delicate stage of life when all those things I mentioned had taken root and I'd come to believe somehow that I just wasn't enough. I had such burning ambitions but I had developed limiting beliefs that trained me to suppress my voice because if I spoke up or pursued my dreams I'd look silly or be proved wrong – I'd tell myself it wasn't going to happen so don't even try. I looked for validation in all the wrong places with no idea of the incredible power I had in me the whole time. And without even realising, my eating disorder developed, although it would take me twelve years to even recognise that was what it was.

Food became both an incredible comfort and a way to soothe myself – the lower I felt, the more I would binge to try and fill myself back up, to fill the void. Then in the same instance it became horribly punishing. The bingeing gave validation to all my fears that I was indeed weak and pathetic, not worthy or deserving of anything else. It became an awful way that I would put myself back in my place, back down where I belonged. And then the punishment would come in the form of purging. I would gain a small sense of control back but then the cycle would start all over again and I became trapped in a dangerous loop with a silent bully. This would go on for twelve years before I got the help I needed, and we'll come back to that later in the chapter.

I've asked you to reflect back on times when you've drawn on your courage. However small or insignificant it may seem here and now, I want to share some of mine. It's these small acts of bravery that have all come together to shape and ultimately change the path of my life. More importantly they have had a significant impact on others and left a mark of what I have to offer the world.

One of the first times I can remember really summoning up courage to help serve others was back when I was eighteen years old. I was working part time in a nursing home whilst taking Business Studies at college. It was a private nursing home, so our very low hourly rate was decided by the owners rather than the NHS. We started to lose a lot of staff to other places paying better money, leaving more work to do and less of us to do it. The atmosphere became strained and, in the end, it was the residents who were suffering. There was lots of moaning, but no one was taking any action as there was "no point" and so I decided to write a letter to the company to try and make a change.

Perhaps it is no big deal to a lot of people, but for me as an eighteen-year-old and the youngest person working there it felt huge. I set to work and passionately wrote out my case for why we as carers deserved better pay and why the residents in turn deserved better service. I remember standing in the lounge reading it out to my Mum, feeling kind of silly but also really proud at the same time. She gave me the extra push and confidence I needed to take it in and get signatures of support from all the staff.

It met some resistance from some of the longer standing members: they told me I was wasting my time and that things would never change. Looking back, I wonder if perhaps they wish they'd tried to do something about it themselves. I wanted to try and make a difference and that burning desire to speak up and take action took over and despite feeling like I might get rejected and look foolish, it seemed worth it and I felt proud of what I was attempting to achieve. Shaking with nerves, I handed in the letter to the Matron and to my surprise she seemed impressed. "It takes guts to do something like this," she told me with a smile. That for me was enough. Being told we are brave is an incredible thing. We all want to have "guts" and we always admire those that do – I now fell into that category and it felt fabulous.

The next month it was announced that we would be getting a pay rise and a better overtime rate. It wasn't huge but it made a difference and although it wasn't acknowledged that my letter was the catalyst, I got lovely comments and thanks from the rest of the staff and I left work that day with a spring in my step. What I said and did mattered, and it could make a difference to others. Courage had paid off.

By the time I was twenty-four life was in a bit of a mess. After graduating with my HND in Business Studies I got a job with a telecommunications company which would pay for my exams to become a qualified accountant. This still makes me chuckle now as it was probably one of the worst choices of career to suit my personality and skill set! I recognise now that I chose this path for status and to prove that I was good enough, smart enough. But I found it rigid and restrictive. I struggled with the exams, even failing one of them and I often made mistakes in my daily work. So ironically, all this did was validate the limiting beliefs I'd try to rebel against in the first place and it simply showed me that, just as suspected, I wasn't good enough and I was a fool for trying.

Out of work, behind closed doors my eating disorder had become all-consuming as I battled with constant anxiety and depression. I was in an unhealthy relationship and I was running up debt by compulsively spending on credit cards. Buying clothes, holidays, meals out that I couldn't afford but that, much like the bingeing with food, temporarily made me feel better about myself. I shut my eyes to what was mounting up until one day (once again in the bath!) I had my very first experience of suicidal thoughts. They were fleeting and I didn't really recognise that's even what they were at the time, but about a week later I woke up with a burning urgency to change everything. It felt like life or death and then, almost as if it was sent from the universe that day, I saw an advert in the local paper for an open day at Southampton University for student nurses.

I arranged to go along, and to cut a long story short, I applied and got accepted for the three-year course to become a registered nurse. It felt like coming home when I got that news – I knew that was where I belonged. I quit my job, ended my relationship and moved into nursing accommodation and once again got a part time job back in a nursing home. I felt exhilarated! In a short space of time I'd completely changed my life – once again courage had paid off and I felt really proud of myself.

My three years at university were a roller coaster. I took to nursing like a duck to water, I got fantastic grades in my written assignments and glowing reports on every practical placement I did. However, debt still plagued me and I had no way of paying it off. I was now working two part time jobs around my full time study, in the nursing home doing night shifts and for a mobile bar at weekends, but barely making ends meet. Lack of money was getting me down and my eating disorder was still rife. By now I was in a happy relationship and the future looked bright as I came to the end of my course and was starting to make plans for moving in together, a trip to Australia and my new career as a nurse. Three months before I qualified, he ended the relationship and I fell into a pit of heartbreak. The world felt like it had ended, and it was once again more validation that I wasn't enough. My health took a nosedive, I stopped eating, I was drinking too much alcohol and my hair started falling out in clumps. Once again a heavy depression took me over me.

One day I went over to my Mum's house feeling tearful, and she came to greet me on the garden path with a hug. She said some simple words but with such conviction in my ear as she gave me the tightest squeeze: "It's his loss, do you hear me? It's his loss." It's funny what triggers us, isn't it? At that moment it was like I remembered who I was and what I was made of. That moment set me free and loss and hopelessness suddenly presented itself as massive opportunity and out charged my inner warrior like never before.

I went online and found a voluntary project in a rural area of Ghana where my nursing skills could be used in the HIV clinic and the malaria ward in the hospital there. There was also the opportunity to help at the local school and orphanage, both of which were in a desperate state.

My heart lit up and I knew it was where I needed to be! There was just one problem: it would cost me six hundred pounds for my flight and the home stay, and I was over five thousand pounds in debt with two maxed out credit cards.

Now, the amazing thing about allowing your burning desire to take over and letting courage kick in is that often, without even knowing it, you draw on all the things you forget (or simply don't believe) you have. Your unique intelligence, intuition, resourcefulness, resilience and creativity can suddenly appear. I used all of these and decided I would raise the money by asking people to sponsor me for a challenge. Even that filled me with fear but I wanted to go so badly that I knew I had to be bold if I was going to get what I wanted so I felt the fear and did it anyway.

I chose The Great London Run which was completely out of my comfort zone and something I'd have to train hard for in a short space of time. Friends and family happily contributed and even asked their friends to as well. I had lots of lovely messages of support and it felt wonderful. I did the training and I ran 10k, which for me was a huge achievement.

After the excitement and adrenalin of completing the run and raising the money died down, reality kicked in and the enormity of what I was about to do hit me. I was going to travel alone and live somewhere completely unknown – fear began to kick in. I can remember sitting on the plane with so much thinking time to myself, knowing there was no turning back.

When I arrived, my first seventy-two hours were incredibly disorganised and uncertain. I felt out of my depth and I wanted to book a flight and return to the comfort and safety of home. But I didn't. Instead I thought about how brave I'd been to make this decision in the first place, what I'd done to get there and more importantly how I'd feel if I gave up now.

I realised then how much I needed this experience and what a huge opportunity for personal growth it could be for me if I let it be. So I stayed. And over the weeks that followed the experiences I had and the people I met touched my heart and changed my life. I lived with no electricity or hot water and slept with cockroaches. Between the hospital, the school and the orphanage I saw some heart-breaking sights and heard some extremely sad stories. But I also met some of the happiest, most inspiring people with the biggest hearts and a totally different outlook on life. They taught me so much about perspective and priorities. In my time there I also made a difference. A big difference, in fact, and I did that by simply being there and being me. By letting all my qualities shine through and the love pour out with no limiting beliefs weighing me down. The best thing about feeling the fear and doing something anyway is that we prove ourselves wrong and we change our story.

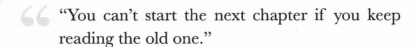

"You can't start the next chapter if you keep reading the old one."

— MICHAEL MCMILLAN

By the time I reached twenty-nine I was still doing exactly that in one area of my life – I was telling myself the same old story and the ending was never changing. After twelve years of a long, confusing battle with myself (made all the more exhausting by the fact it was a secret battle), suicidal thoughts once again finally opened my eyes to the fact I'd hit rock bottom mentally.

And so back to that moment I mentioned earlier when I was sat the bath feeling there was no point to my life. I was in such a dark place that I truly believed that the world and particularly the people who loved me would be better off without me – I was just a burden and I didn't deserve to be here.

It's emotional for me to write this looking back now, because of course I know that wasn't true, but also because to the outside world I appeared as quite the opposite. You see, I was confident and bold, I grabbed life by the horns, and I had lots of friends. No one would have believed what my life looked like behind closed doors, something I think that stopped me getting help and kept me trapped for longer. Because actually there was always that little warrior inside: alongside the scared little girl was a very brave one, with a big voice and unstoppable determination – I just didn't listen to her as much as I should have. And it was she that came through when I needed her the most and led me to make what was still to this day the bravest move of my life and get some help.

I can still remember sitting outside the counsellor's house fifteen minutes early for my appointment and that wait felt like fifteen years. Fear nearly got the better of me. I felt terrified and totally alone. But again, she rose, that wonderful brave inner fighter and in we went - and everything changed.

It took three months and things felt worse before they got better. Courage was needed each week to return to the sessions to uncover things I didn't want to look at and to say things I wanted to leave unsaid. But what happened over that time was that all those limiting beliefs I had and monumental fears that had built up started to lose their power. That strong, confident brave girl inside me became more and more empowered and I came away from that time knowing more than ever that my voice is meant to be heard. I am worthy and I have so much to share with the world and serve others with.

From that time to now life hasn't been plain sailing by any means. I suffered post-natal depression after having both of my incredible baby boys, I've lost my beautiful Nan who was one of my best friends and I've been through a divorce. Life hasn't got easier, but I've got stronger and more often than not I choose joy. Over the years I've proved I have the courage to make bold decisions that can lead to big changes. I know that limiting beliefs are exactly that and I can recognise whether my thoughts are serving me or sabotaging me. These days I trust my inner warrior and let her be my guide – she is always the one who makes the magic happen when she's let loose and so now I let her run the show. As a result, my life is heading in a whole new direction.

Over the past two and a half years, after having the courage to take a leap of faith and a chance on myself, I have built a very successful Network Marketing business in the travel industry. So far I have helped over one thousand people to get started on their own journey as a business owner. I've been able to use my own story to inspire and empower others to know that they can do the same. I'm now able to help people change the path of their life and work towards personal, financial and time freedom and create a lifestyle that serves them.

I am creating the wealth that I know I deserve and the choices that serve me and my family. Most importantly, I am showing my boys that their Mum can do anything she puts her mind to (including being an author!) and that so can they.

And so can you. After reading my story, if there is one thing that stays with you, I would love it to be this:

If you have ideas and dreams, however big or small, they are there for a reason. When you leave your dreams and desires unmet, when you don't fulfil your purpose, you feel it because it stays with you. Left for too long, I believe you end up feeling unfulfilled, swamped in limiting beliefs and in some cases even depressed.

Whatever you've told yourself about why you can't change careers, write that book, design that product, grow that business, take that trip or start up that charity – it's time to change the story. If you've convinced yourself that you're not smart enough, worthy enough or deserving enough, not influential enough, you don't have the time or the finance, then let this be the moment you replace those beliefs with these instead...

You have everything you need inside you right now to create anything you desire. You are so powerful if only you will let yourself be. You deserve to live a life of abundance with a fire alight inside you. You don't need to stop feeling fear, you simply need to choose courage to overcome it so that you can say yes to opportunity and go and grab everything that was meant for you.

Never again say that you can't because actually... you can.

ABOUT THE AUTHOR

SARAH BOULTER

Sarah Boulter is an award-winning Network Marketer who has built a hugely successful business within the travel industry. She is also the founder of Happy Living with Sarah and full-time mum to her two boys, Freddie and Leo.

Sarah built up her venture whilst a stay at home mum and now, as she continues to build a six-figure business, her mission is to empower many others to do the same. To date she has helped over one thousand people to start their own journey using the vehicle of a network marketing business, helping them strive for personal, financial and time freedom.

Sarah's passion lies in coaching and she uses both her business and her social media platforms to inspire and empower others to pursue their dreams and create the lifestyle they deserve.

You can connect with Sarah at:

facebook.com/happylivingsarahsbiz

instagram.com/happy_livingwithsarah

SOPHIE POWELL

> *"Be who you are and say what you feel, because those who mind don't matter, and those who matter don't mind."*

— *BERNARD M. BARUCH*

*W*hen we are children, we are free to live in the land of imagination. One where you can be anything you choose to be. It may be as the princess living at the top of the castle, or in a land of unicorns and sparkles. It's a place you feel safe to be you, unapologetically, where nobody can judge you.

Unfortunately, as we get older, our safe haven no longer serves its purpose and things can feel a lot more complicated. In an uphill struggle of survival, we find ourselves reaching for the mindset books and other personal development resources to help guide us.

From my own experiences as a child, I was living in a land that made me happy, and it had lots of sparkles. However, I did have my own obstacles to overcome even then. We anticipate that when we are older we will have it all figured out. If only it was as simple and as easy as that. Truth is, no matter how many disastrous times you have gone through, no matter how many times you have had to overcome adversity and pick yourself back up, no matter how many times people have tried to keep you living in a box of how they think you 'should' be living, it's your birthright to ignore them. You can do and be anything you want to! And I fully support you.

Life can continue to throw lemons: I know because I have been there too and I hope this chapter can come as a reassuring message that you aren't alone and we can get through any lemon, hurdle, challenge, and obstacle that comes our way. It is my deepest desire that my chapter inspires you to feel confident to be YOU. This will be my biggest gift to you.

> "Happiness can be found, even in the darkest of times, if one only remembers to turn on the light."
>
> — J.K. ROWLING

For a very long time I struggled with happiness. As a child I can honestly look back and say I was happy. However, I did live with the struggles of dyspraxia (a form of development disorder of the brain), which caused me to struggle in any activities that required coordination and movement. On top of this I struggled with dyslexia. Both of these made me feel very different from other children. For most children, they can expect to start walking at the age of one, and usually start talking around this age too. For me, unfortunately, it wasn't quite the same. It took me a lot longer with interventions such as speech therapy, physiotherapy and hydrotherapy to support me. The consequences of all of this left me feeling tired, exhausted, and drained most of the time. However, I continued on and eventually built up the strength to walk. As you can imagine, none of this was easy on me or my family. Back then, there was really limited awareness of what dyspraxia even was, and for most people it wasn't even heard of. Apparently, it is believed to affect ten percent of the population, while two percent are estimated to be severely affected by the condition. Like I mentioned, it wasn't an easy ride but we made the best of it. I remember fabulous family trips and childhood memories that were always surrounded with love from the people around me. As grateful as I am for all of this, I still lived with this knowing that I was just a bit different from anyone else.

Overcoming this was the start of many hurdles that life continued to throw at me. When I look back now, feeling different must have impacted my self-worth because I allowed negative people and relationships into my world easily. In my early twenties I fell into the trap of loving a narcissist (although I didn't know it at the time!).

During the first couple of years we were both happy with each other in many ways. We did all of the things that couples do, but it didn't last. After a few years, it was almost as if a dark cloud came over him and changed his world, with me right at the heart of it. Truth was, back then I didn't see it. When we love someone that much it can blind us from the truth. I remember the aggression gradually starting. At first it was just verbal but it felt so crippling, like he had taken over my mind and was inside of me. He was able to tap into all of my fears and deepest insecurities. Then the possessive behaviour, to the point where I wasn't allowed to do anything, and if I did there would be consequences.

Over time, my life, my soul, my world literally felt like it was being sucked out of me, and worst of all, I was allowing it to happen, feeling paralysed to do anything about it. Following this I fell pregnant but I lost it at five months. It was all due to the stress and abuse I had endured and I remember feeling rock bottom. Like Jekyll and Hyde, from one moment of abuse, to the next a moment of love, I then received a proposal with promises of the abuse never happening again.

Of course, this didn't end up to be the truth and I continued to allow years more of abuse, control and feeling rock bottom with no self-worth. Amongst the whirlwind of all that this relationship had already brought me, I was blessed to fall pregnant for the second time, but like the first time, I lost it. He had been carrying on with other women, was losing interest in me completely until one day he ended it all. I remember feeling so many emotions. I thank him to this day for walking away and allowing me to find myself again. They always say you will never forget what someone said, but you will always remember how they made you feel. I felt my lowest low, yet still remember one thing he said to me: "I am nothing and worth nothing." Ouch. I totally believed it too.

Although I had escaped, my life did continue to crumble around me. I ended up with severe depression for quite some time and there were times I genuinely remember feeling like it would be easier to end it all. However, I did start seeing my therapist to support me in overcoming what had been some really dark moments. For anyone who has endured times of depression you will know how it feels too. Anxiety was another real player in my life back then. I completely lost sight of who I even was. Have you ever felt like that?

I remember just feeling completely numb. Everything felt like hard work and I had moments of panic and hyperventilating which turned into the most horrific panic attacks.

This was a frequent occurrence for me, and at the time I wasn't working so social interaction was pretty limited. I felt lonely. Even though I had wonderful people supporting me which I will be forever grateful for, inside it was an immense feeling of loneliness.

I was thinking over and over, why me? How did I get here? What am I doing here? What is the point of me being here? At this time, I felt there was just no point. I was emotionally, physically and mentally exhausted.

People used to say a lot of things to help me see the light: 'Time's a healer; you can get through this; everything happens for a reason.' I respected so much of what they were saying and knew the intention was to make me feel better but quite honestly, I wanted to reject it because it just reminded me of how lost and broken I really was. I felt completely trapped and I really didn't know what to do. Many thoughts used to run through my head, and I tried many things to help me feel better, most of which failed and left me feeling angry, worthless and a nobody. I was actually scared of how I felt about myself and my life and knew things needed to change before it was too late.

They say when you hit rock bottom the only way is up and I guess this is true for me too. I remember waking up one day and something just clicking inside of me. At the time I couldn't tell you what. It was just like I was given a second chance of life. The opportunity to reignite the spark in me, and connect back to who I really was, which for so long had felt missing. I wanted to find me, but I also held back through fear of not meeting the expectation others had of me.

Over the last few years, I have been on an incredible journey of finding myself, one that has led me to the path that always has been true to me. I am happier than I have ever been. I am now married to my husband who treats me like a queen. I have completely come off medication and no longer have panic attacks in the way that I used to. More than that, I feel confident to be unapologetically me because I know that it's my real answer to true happiness.

Have you ever felt that you can be and do more? Or ever felt like you just want to be more like yourself?

When you are trying to be anything else but you, it can feel like you are betraying who you really are. But the truth is, it takes time to get to know oneself. It takes time to heal from past wounds. It takes allowing yourself to go on a journey of self-discovery to really fulfil your true purpose and potential. It takes hard work, facing old demands and having the courage to trust in yourself and your own intuition.

When I first met my husband, I was still recovering from everything from my past. I remember telling him every-thing that had been my world for so long even on our very first date. I thought he must have thought I was mad, but in truth I felt comfortable for the very first time, telling my story and my truth. It enabled me to accept what had been and close many doors that were no longer serving me. There was no judgment and, in that moment, I remember feeling free to be me. So, for anyone who is holding on to struggles from their past, when you can find that friend or person to openly share your struggles with, it can support you in so many ways. My honesty and openness actually led him to want to be with me (who would have known it!). He didn't run a mile! In fact, our energy and connection was something even to this day I can't put into words. Everyone has those moments but you have to feel it to be able to know.

> "It is not how much we have, but how much we enjoy, that makes happiness."
>
> — CHARLES SPURGEON

Opening up and expressing how I felt at the time truly helped me to heal. It helped me in ways I never thought it could. When you release something that you have been carrying around for so long, it makes you feel like you can breathe again. It's liberating! For anyone reading this that can resonate with any of my story, maybe there are things you are ready to let go of too? Of course, self-discovery and healing is never a straight road, but one I promise will shape your world forever more. In the same way that I have, you can find your happy place, your voice and your confidence to be you, unapologetically. My message to you is to never be afraid to speak your truth, say what you mean and love yourself enough to follow what feels good for you.

My connection to the universe has also hugely developed as a result of this. One thing I know for sure, is that the universe always has a plan for us. Sometimes our lowest lows become our highest blessings, and the storms create our sunshine. Everything can become a lesson and a blessing leading us to the path that is meant for us. I had to hit rock bottom to find my feet but I will be forever grateful for my journey because it really has been what's enabled me to find my own wings. Of course, I wish I could have helped myself sooner than I did but my journey was my journey and has enabled me to become the woman I am today. Just know, wherever you are in your life, whatever challenges, past demands or situations are currently causing you pain, you can do this too.

As grateful as I am for my life, I know there will always be lemons and to add to what had already been a roller coaster of a ride, back in 2018 I was diagnosed with fibromyalgia. This condition is often caused by stressful events, including physical or emotional (psychological) stress so it sounded about right for me, someone who has endured pretty much all of that to the extreme! With it came a whole heap of new challenges. The pain it inflicts is one that can often take your breath away. It's a pain through my body that before then I had never experienced. I am able to manage this much better today and to be honest that really has been the result of the personal development and mindset work I have done to work on myself over the last however many years so for that I am forever grateful. The mind really is a powerful thing! I am able to ride the wave of pain through breathing techniques and controlling my holistic approach, as I feel if you can manage without medication then do it.

As much as I value medication, I remember feeling like I wanted to do this on my own and be in control. I exercised more, went on long walks, attempted Yoga (even though I am definitely not a natural!) and did as much as I could to stretch my muscles and keep me healthy. When I look back now, I really did handle it like a pro, because I knew I wasn't going to let this lemon get to me like I had many things in the past. I was resilient and wanted to keep on top. So, if you are currently going through anything similar, keep your head above water, look at what you can control and remember how powerful you are. We can't choose what happens to us but we can absolutely choose how we respond to what happens to us. Be ready for down days, they are inevitable, but you also have the power to live your life to the fullest despite any health challenges in your way. Keep your mind and perspective strong and you will stay strong. There is so much in the world for me to still see and do, like there is for you too. I now choose to be happy despite my health ailments and choose to embrace every opportunity with open arms to reach my potential and feel truly happy. If I can, after every up and down, I know you can too.

So now I come to the end of my journey to date, I share with you my current reality. For a while now my husband and I have been longing for that one thing that is missing from our life to be totally complete. You have guessed it right, a baby. Knowing that I once had two pregnancies, to now not anything has been a tough pill to swallow. There have been many times I've blamed myself wondering why, as our tests don't show any answer as to what the problem has been. I remember sitting in the Gynaecology office and being told it's just 'unexplained infertility.'

I felt like this was almost worse as it gave us no answers. It took me a long time to process our reality in all honesty. I wanted the solution. This is the normal progress of life, right? Getting married, having children and being a family. In reality, one in five couples go through infertility so although I am not on my own, it can sure feel like a lonely place to be. I have developed many coping strategies to support me through any baby moments. I used to be triggered by people announcing they were pregnant on social media, or being invited to baby showers, and just feeling uncomfortable around babies. I know it might sound mad, but it was my truth and my reality for a long time. Before I had worked on myself with strategies to support me, my emotions used to be all over the place. For anyone reading this who has been through something similar, hopefully my message is resonating with you.

Maybe you too have found yourself bursting into tears at the sight of pregnant women wondering what's wrong with you? It's a push, pull feeling because on one hand you want to be happy for everyone else but inside it just makes you feel angry, resentful and sad that it's not happening for you too. Until you experience it, I know it can feel hard to understand what it's truly like. People used to tell me to just relax and let it happen naturally… to a degree, yes, relaxing is a great and useful tool. However, it's easier said than done.

Nowadays, I do feel there is so much pressure on becoming pregnant by a certain age and the media is a continuous reminder of women becoming pregnant and being mums. I often see women in their 40s, 50s and even 60s having children, all of which is wonderful for them but quite often has left me wondering what the hell is wrong with me? I am thirty: surely I should be able to? However, over time I have really come to terms with where we are and I am over the moon to be soon undertaking our first cycle of IVF. Scary? Sure!

For a long time, this route did make me feel like a failure because I couldn't do it on my own. With no explanation you almost feel like there is never any closure. If you can resonate with any of my messages, you will know what I mean when I say this process can leave you feeling disconnected from everyone around you. There have been times I have completely wanted to shut down because I don't expect anyone else to understand the heartache this can feel like. However, like I said, I am feeling so positive now and am so incredibly grateful that we have this opportunity for IVF. I hope one day soon I can look back at this chapter as the Mum I know I want to be, but for now I sit in complete gratitude that we are making progress to where we want to be. In the light of all that has happened to me, the miracle of it all it made me realise my big purpose, my big why for being here, which is to help other women going through this fertility process and now I can confidently give them the mindset, the resources, the emotional, physical and spiritual support to give them the very best chance of success, which is where I am at now in my own life.

As I look into the future, not just for myself, but for all of us, it's true that we can be where we want to be whilst being true to who we really are. My life circumstances could have broken me but I have instead allowed it to make me. Through personal development and investing time to find me, I am a much more positive person than I ever thought I could be. I have found my voice and fully appreciate what it means to be unapologetically me. I feel stronger than I could ever know, and braver than I could ever think, and this is how I wish for you to feel too. Don't ever put yourself down or allow others to dictate your self-worth. Show the world who you are and never be afraid of shining your own light.

Being you is the most powerful thing you can be. From my own experiences I have learnt that I can't be anyone else and feel truly happy. I have learned to protect my energy from those who don't serve me and built my resilience to overcome all of the lemons that may lay ahead before me. Writing this chapter has been a really positive part of that journey and I thank you as the reader for giving me this space to share my truth and share my world and I hope it inspired you to do the same for you too.

Whatever has happened in your life, embrace every hurdle with new possibilities and choose to create your reality, not be dictated to by what anyone else thinks or says. The woman who got you to where you are today may not be the woman you need to become to take you where you want to get to and that's OK too. It's about finding the strength to grow, learn and overcome what's necessary to step into her shoes. It goes without saying that the only way from the bottom is up.

> *"I believe in being strong when everything seems to be going wrong. I believe that happy girls are the prettiest girls. I believe that tomorrow is another day, and I believe in miracles."*
>
> — *AUDREY HEPBURN*

Imagine how it would feel to have the power to overcome every hurdle every day like the superwoman that you are? Honestly, if you had told me all of those years ago that I would be standing as the woman I am today I would've never believed you. My journey has been my own and it's been perfectly imperfect to bring me to where I am today. So, what does your imperfect journey look like to you? However you get to your true self, know it's OK to be you. When life throws you lemons, remember to focus on what you can control, and what you can't, well… just learn to let that go and take each day as it comes and when you look back at the dots you will be surprised with just how far you have come.

My journey will continue and will be changing on a daily basis. It doesn't matter where we come from, who we are and what beliefs we have. We are all in this world together. I have a belief that I am being guided in every possible way. I was meant to go through what I have been through in order for me to be the woman I am today. Whatever belief that you may have, don't be afraid of showing it, don't be ashamed of how your past cultivated the life you are living now. Never be afraid of your failures, the negative relationships that stole your self-worth, the opportunities you missed or people you let go of. Your journey was meant for you.

Remember that little girl that's inside of you - the inner child. You have been protecting her from the pain that is your past. It's OK to let it go, it's OK to take away that pain, all the stress, tears and drama that no longer serves you. Know you have come so far and you deserve so much to be happy. Even on the cloudiest and dullest of days the sun is still shining and it's always going to be there with you no matter what you are going through.

We all have that inner strength inside us and you can be anything and do anything you want to. The most important thing to do is remember who you are and look how far you have come. Follow your heart and do what you've set out to do.

If I have learnt anything from my own journey, it's that I am capable and I have so much passion and love for myself. I've never admitted anything like this before and it really surprises me how far I have come. That time of getting to know myself and listening to what my needs are is a beautiful journey. I'm looking forward to all the possibilities that will come my way and I am ready to take on any challenges that will come my way too. Be ready for the world in as many ways as you can because women are capable of anything.

Be brave, be strong and know you are a powerful being. Look after you and when you are ready you can let go of the past and look forward to the future. I will be with you every step of the way. If I can do it, you can all do it. We all deserve happiness, to live our dreams, to look back and be proud of how far we have come and to be confident within ourselves. Take a deep breath, let it out and know it's time to shine.

"A strong woman loves, forgives, walks away, lets go, tries again, and perseveres ... no matter what life throws at her."

Thank you for giving me this space to share my truth, my world and my reality. I hope it encourages you to share your truth, be who you are, and live life to the fullest.

ABOUT THE AUTHOR

SOPHIE POWELL

Sophie Powell is a Fertility Coach.

Sophie is passionate about helping other women through their fertility journey. After experiencing the struggles herself, she understands how it feels. After working on her mindset through spiritual, emotional and physical release she is now able to help other women around her.

Sophie is on a mission to help globally women through their own fertility and she really appreciates the demands of it all.

Her mission is to help support women who are yearning to be mothers create the very best chance of conceiving, making their dreams come true through spiritual, emotional and physical release.

Contact

Email: Fertilitywithsophie@gmail.com

 facebook.com/sophie.rossp

STACEY KNIGHT-JONES

THE DOTS WILL ALWAYS JOIN IN THE END

"The dots only make sense when you can join them. But they always join in the end."

— REBECCA CAMPBELL

I never set out to be a coach. It wasn't something I woke up one day and knew instinctively was the direction to take. Even as I started to join the dots it wasn't blindingly obvious. I'm not great at seeing what the universe is trying to tell me. It's something which I'm working on but I'm not there yet. So, in all honesty, nothing has ever felt blindingly obvious to begin with. It's only afterwards with reflection and hindsight that I have seen the journey unfold and seen that everything, in fact, has been part of a seemingly imperfect journey.

From one soulful female to another, I want to pause for a moment to thank you for picking up this book today. I have no doubt that the timing is divinely perfect and I am extremely humbled that my words are finding their way from me to you. I don't believe that you finding this book was an accident, rather part of a bigger plan that maybe you are yet to discover.

> *"Shoot for the moon. Even if you miss it you will land among the stars."*
>
> — NORMAN VINCENT PEALE

My hope is that my words also inspire you to allow yourself to dream bigger than you may ever have allowed yourself to before. That you are able to release your inner child. Children have the incredible ability to be able to dream in a way that as adults we seem to lose along the way. Release that inner dancer, that space crusader or famous pop star. I look at my children every day and feel inspired by their resilience, tenacity and ability to grab the world with both hands. Listen to what that inner voice is whispering to you and shoot for the moon.

> *"Realise that the hows and whys will all make sense soon enough."*
>
> — MIKE DOOLEY

Let's start from the beginning…

Do you ever have that feeling that you know there's something you are missing? That little niggle that you can't shake off? I've heard people say before, mostly in films but in life too, often when the going gets tough, *"There's got to be more to life than this!"*

Maybe, just like I have, you are searching for something. Maybe you don't know what that something is yet. Maybe you feel you have lost direction. Maybe you feel completely alone right now. Or you feel unsupported in the pursuit of your dreams. Maybe you simply don't know what you want any more or you don't know how to take action. Maybe, like I did for oh, so long, you feel guilty for wanting more than you have. Maybe you live in fear of what others think of you.

Wherever you are at, whatever you may be experiencing, I hope that my words in this chapter help you to shine bright, because you deserve to live the life you always dreamed of. Your own life by design.

> *"To the mind that is still, the whole universe surrenders."*
>
> — LAO TZU

I always knew there was something more to life. It was almost impossible to hear, like a faint whisper in the breeze. But I could never shake that feeling that something was missing. A piece of the puzzle still to be found, something that was much bigger than me. Something I was yet to understand.

I thought that it was just part of growing up and that it would all somehow just unravel and become clear one day. That feeling led me down a path of spirituality that is still very much unfolding in its own sweet time, but a path that has both supported and inspired my journey into entrepreneurism. I still wince a little as I write the word 'entrepreneur'. It makes it seem like I have everything all figured out, that I intended to be on this path and everything worked out to a conscious, intentional plan.

The truth is that I don't think we can ever truly know the definitive 'hows', and in this chapter I will actually share with you how it's absolutely OK to, in fact, not have a clue what the 'hows' are. The only thing I know for sure is that my vision for life is so crystal clear that I am willing to stop at nothing to get there. I know what my life will look like if I don't achieve my vision, and I know to the point of obsession what my life will look like when I get there.

When I first started my entrepreneurial journey back in 2011 after the birth of my beautiful first child I knew then, like never before, that I wanted to create a life for him that was abundant in excitement, beautiful memories and so many 'yes' moments (moments without compromise). I had been blessed with a beautiful boy who had chosen me to be his Mummy, his guide and his beacon. I wanted to show up for him, to be there for everything that was important to him and to be the very best version of me whilst doing that.

I had set the bar high but I knew that I wouldn't ever give up. I would fight every single day. I knew with every cell of my being I was going to stop at nothing to make it happen. As Alex Williams said on the popular Netflix series 'Suits', *"It's not my job to show them [his children] how the world is, but how the world should be."* And I intended to live by this from the moment they were born.

With little other than a burning desire to be a work from home Mummy and a bag full of dreams, I embarked on my second business in June 2012. I was encouraged by my introducer to think about what I truly wanted from starting the business, why I wanted to travel a road less trodden, and when the going got tough (which it did) what did I want reminding of to keep me going. Back then my son was just eleven months old but my dream was to be at his first sports day and every one after that and to never have to ask permission to be there for him. My financial target was just £600 a month. That's all I needed in order to be able to stay at home and not have to return to my day job.

Back then I was working as a primary school teaching assistant, and although at first it was my dream job inspiring all of those young minds, I felt that there was another pull. It wasn't just about being home with my son either. There was something much bigger at play. I would tire of hearing others making small talk about other staff members or how unfairly they were being treated. It would make me want to almost wake them up to what was out there for them to grab with both hands, but I knew that people only see when they are ready so I would smile politely and think about the vision of my perfect day.

The target seemed so achievable, so doable and as I saw the possibilities mounting, I couldn't help but feel incredibly excited! Excited that my plan B would soon become my plan A. Excited that I was surrounding myself with people who thought outside of the box and spoke about their hopes and dreams and most importantly, would encourage me to do the same too!

66 *"Live the Life of Your Dreams: Be brave enough to live the life of your dreams according to your vision and purpose instead of the expectations and opinions of others."*

— ROY T. BENNETT

Fast forward a few months and I had vomited the business over my friends and family, with varying degrees of success (not all too bad). I realised that I had zero knowledge of how to actually grow my business with integrity and poise, and to make matters worse I had entered the world of social media and company incentives. I had begun to lose my own vision of success. Before I knew it my vision board was full of experiences, numbers, possessions and titles, that were so far off course from what I actually wanted that I started to lose focus. All I wanted was to be able to stay at home with my children. Instead I was sucked into a world that wasn't where I was meant to be, reaching for things I didn't want.

I couldn't see it, but because this vision was not real, it wasn't mine, ultimately my energy shifted and I found myself in complete misalignment. I started to feel like I was failing at everything. I didn't hit the targets I had set; I started to doubt and second guess absolutely everything I did. Not only did this affect my business but my life too. I started to develop anxiety around even the most simple of tasks. I even had an episode when I was so incredibly stressed that I felt like I had lost time, that time was repeating itself and I was so worried about not remembering to pick my son up from school one day that I had to set an alarm. It was a time I wouldn't wish to repeat.

So I invite you to just take a moment to check in. Is your vision your version of success? Does it truly reflect what YOU really want? Have you been swayed by what you think others want of you? Have you been swayed by how you believe you SHOULD be, not what you actually wish to be?

> *"If you want to have enough to give to others, you will need to take care of yourself first. A tree that refuses water and sunlight for itself can't bear fruit for others."*

— EMILY MAROUTIAN

Let's talk about guilt for a moment. The guilt is real, it's crippling, it's debilitating, and throw in a measure of imposter syndrome and a sprinkle of comparisonitis and boy, oh boy! At times I have wondered why I put myself through it all: the frustration, the bleak days of attempting to balance time, trying to be the best mum I can be to my children, the best wife and business owner too. Trying so desperately to figure it all out, make a respectable income and provide for my family. Not to mention, being my own version of success. Sometimes I would literally feel like I was dying on the inside, trapped in a web of confusion and frustration. A lost chaotic mess.

In 2015 I remember distinctly my daughter was just a few months old. She was delivered by emergency caesarean under general anaesthetic. It was rather a frightening time and the recovery was incredibly tough, especially as my son was just four. I was also incredibly tough on myself too. I had made the decision that 2016 was the year that I would be fully financially supported by my business and that I would be leaving my job as a primary school teaching assistant. So the pressure was on to not only keep my business moving over the coming months but to actually grow the business to support that decision. I was set in my head to really move mountains and then all of a sudden, BAM! It hit me, out of nowhere, without warning, without invitation. In fact it was rather rude!

I lost my identity.

Honestly, don't laugh here. Sure, I had roles: I was Mummy, I was wife, I was business owner. But WHO was I REALLY? What was I doing this all for? Did I even know WHY I was doing it? What was the end goal?

I knew I needed to be living my passions, but what in the world were they? I knew I needed to be looking after me. But WHAT did I enjoy? How did I like to spend my time?

I couldn't answer ANY of those questions. And I'll be honest, it wasn't a great feeling. If, as you read this right now, and any of that resonates with you, first of all I want you to know that you are SO not alone, and secondly yes, it's very normal.

The great news is that you don't have to continue feeling this way forever. I lived in the dark for so many years, never knowing who I was deep down, not hearing my true voice and not seeing how I wanted to truly show up in this world and the difference I wanted to make.

"Only after your first step can you begin to take your second. Do something—do anything!"

— MIKE DOOLEY

I have always been an action taker, and I've always believed that if something isn't serving you, bringing you joy, or lighting you up, then you absolutely have the choice to do something about it. When I left school I had six jobs and four college courses all in the space of about two years. I also did half a degree before finding myself in a very dark place so I walked away from that too. And I will let you into a little secret if I may. I have also had not one but seven different businesses!

I tell you this because as a coach, and in fact as someone who has networked with women-only groups for over eight years, I come across women all of the time who are either unhappy in their current business or who wish to develop their business slightly differently to how they have previously operated, and they are fearful. Fearful mostly about what others will think about them. And I get it! I too would believe that I couldn't change my business, not AGAIN, for fear of what others would say. I would worry they would think I was a quitter, or afraid to work hard. But the truth is, it doesn't really matter what others may or may not think. This is your life and you owe it to yourself to feel complete inner happiness and joy in what you do and who you choose to work with.

And where is the rule book to all of this? I don't ever recall reading anything which states once you have tried something you have to stick with it: that's it... game over! Businesses grow and develop, U-turn, re-brand, re-market. You name it, they do it, all of the time. The difference is, we very often don't hear about it. We only get to see the good bits, the bits that people want us to hear. And this in itself contributes to another very distorted understanding of the world. As business owners, we believe that we have to be polished, a fountain of knowledge, slick, perfection before we can get out there and share our message.

But I believe that you have to take action, often imperfect action, those baby steps in order to find your joy, your purpose, and what you are truly passionate about.

Sometimes it *is* a leap of faith but what I found was that no one was going to give me permission. The perfect storm was never going to come and I had to take action, however scary that seemed. Sure, my inner critic has always been sat there on my shoulder, eager to have her say, but deep down I always knew that my message was stronger, that it was ready to be heard.

"You never fail until you stop trying."

— ALBERT EINSTEIN

When you do begin to take action, it's so incredibly normal to peak and trough with emotions, motivation, and even belief. As a coach I hold the hands and walk beside so many women who have this constant conflict of reaching for their dreams, knowing what they want to create, but having so many inner disputes to contend with along the way. I tell them all the same thing. This is totally normal and you are not alone!

I remember the feeling so well. The crippling frustrations and the tears (oh, so many tears). Knowing that I had all the tools I needed to pave my way but seeming to be standing IN my own way all at the same time. When you embark on creating a life, rather than letting life happen to you, you need to have people around you who can pick you up when you fall, even hold you up before you start to stumble.

I remember feeling guilty because I would shy away from talking to those closest to me about much to do with my business. I would fear their judgement or misunderstanding. I really did not need to in most cases, but I would worry about being caught out in some way. I think, looking back, that I felt I didn't have all of the answers. I was still trying to work it all out, so if they asked me something I couldn't answer I would look weak and like I didn't know what I was doing.

There have been varying points during the growth and development of my business where guilt has struck in different ways too. Sometimes I would be networking my business early evening or taking a training webinar which would mean missing bedtime routine with the children. And although six nights out of seven I would be there, there would always be that pang of guilt that would rise up, especially if there were tears and tantrums.

When the children were really small, there were some-times days when I would literally busy them with toys and T.V. and I would sit at my laptop. And yes, I have also been that Mum in the park who is on my phone whilst they are playing happily and covering themselves with grass. The guilt was present during all of those times too, but what I figured was that those tiny moments in the grand picture have allowed me to be at home, to be the school run Mum and to be at everything that is important to them. The assemblies, the performances, the coffee mornings and oh, so so so so many clubs and parties. I wouldn't change it for the world.

> *"And as she fell apart, her shattered pieces began to bloom — blossoming until she became herself exactly as she was meant to be..."*

— BECCA LEE

We spend most of our lives from childhood trying to 'fit in', to please others and be accepted. Our internal scripts are made up of what we learn and adopt from those who we are around the most, particularly as we are growing up and learning about the world. Often, this can form quite a distorted understanding, and so can throw us quite far off track.

I remember when I was about six years old, we had to copy huge chunks of writing from the chalk board at school. We had to write it in pencil and we weren't allowed to rub out any mistakes as the teacher wanted to see them. I always liked to try my best and my writing wasn't as good as I felt it needed to be (it makes me quite sad to think of my six year old self worrying about being perfect). One particular day I made a mistake and my friend pointed out that if I licked my finger and rubbed at the pencil slightly it would rub out. I rubbed too hard and made a hole in the page. I recall shaking with fear as I queued at the teacher's desk to show her my finished work, pleading in my head that she wouldn't notice. She did notice. She stopped the whole class and had me hold up my hand. Whilst I stood there sweating, my heart pounding, and looking at the sea of faces staring back at me over the thick oak desk, she told them that I believed that I had rubbers on the end of my fingers. Of course, they laughed. I probably would have done the same. But what she didn't realise was right there in that moment, a moment she probably forgot in an instant, a moment I don't think I will ever forget, she erased something in me I never thought I would get back.

From then on, I worried about making mistakes. I worried that everything I did had to be perfect or else I would be made fun of and become a spectacle for others. That moment manifested and grew into a belief which in turn stunted my creativity. I believed that I wasn't good enough to draw because I was afraid to practise and get it wrong. I believed that it was a bad thing to make mistakes and so I was fearful to try. This is something I have learned to combat and work with, but even into my early 30s I had mindset blocks around being creative. Not just in an arty way, but around creating something from scratch, a course, or a talk, or even a chapter in a book!

I wonder if it wasn't this moment that inspired me to embark on my career path as a primary school teaching assistant, and to subsequently help and support others with Mindset. Joining the dots here, I believe that maybe it was, that there was a deep desire to right a wrong. To ensure that others weren't living with the hurts of the past that had followed them, manifesting and snowballing, encroaching on their life and holding on to them, suffocating their unconscious. It instead allows me to understand the power of words and actions and have empathy and understanding to help others.

> *"Look, if you're going to get better, you have to push yourself. If you push yourself, you're going to fall. If you're not falling, you're not pushing. Falling is part of getting better."*
>
> — DARREN HARDY

What I have found through all of this, and similar mindset stumbles, is the importance of surrounding yourself with those incredible people who you feel are 'Your Tribe', those who cheerlead you. Those with whom, when you're around them, you can just be you. Those who will call you out when you need it (with oodles of love, of course), those who will catch your tears for you, and those who can inspire you to just keep going. I have different people for different moments. I know who to talk to if I need a kick up the bum, I know who to call if I need a straight talking conversation and I know that my coach is always there for motivation and getting back on track. Yep, even the coach has a coach!

There are times when you feel hurt, betrayed, when it's just all too much. These are very often the times when you have started to listen to all of the noise and looked sideways. It's so easy to believe everything we see on social media, or on the latest podcast episode. These platforms are amazing tools, but only when we recognise our own boundaries and triggers.

When I first qualified as a coach and started to share it with the world, my imposter saboteur thought we were besties, I think. She would pop over quite frequently, mostly unannounced and have her say. Mostly things like, 'You don't know what you're doing,' and, 'No one is listening so just give up and go back to the day job, stick to what you know.' Oh, and one of her favourites was always, 'You're not doing it like...... She's WAY better than you, she's got better branding, better engagement, she knows EXACTLY what her client wants, you're just playing at this.'

Resonate?

It hurts; in fact its crippling, isn't it? But you know what? If you know your client is out there somewhere waiting for you, if you know your vision so clearly that you can almost touch it, you have to take a breath, seek the support and guidance you need to press on, and take the action.

> *"The key to realizing a dream is to focus not on success but significance, and then even the small steps and little victories along your path will take on greater meaning."*
>
> — OPRAH WINFREY

This is my journey. I have found this an incredibly difficult story to tell, for many reasons. I have wept whilst writing, both tears of joy and tears of heartbreak. Heartbreak for the young girl whose parents knew nothing of what their daughter experienced for fear of letting them see her faults. Heartbreak for the reflection of her I see in my own children and the protective instincts I feel for them. Heartbreak for the tears I experienced along the way in various chapters of my life, the manifested self-limitations imposed by a distorted understanding of my own abilities. Heartbreak for the unkind words that have echoed around my mind for longer than they are welcome.

Beautiful tears of joy as the healing writing experience has allowed me a deeper opportunity to reflect on the many milestones and conquered quests I have achieved.

This is how my dots have joined so far. I have no doubt that there will be more dots to join as I continue to travel this road of self-discovery we call life. My journey has taught me so many valuable lessons and has lit fires within me that cannot be doused. It is these fires and passions that have driven me to work with women who, just like me, feel the calling to seek clarity and confidence to make sense of their dreams, desires and inner whispers.

As a Clarity Coach, I walk beside my clients. We discover, we unpick, and we look inwards, and together, as I guide, we take those all-important action steps to bring their dreams into reality.

You see, through joining my dots I am able to bring an empathy to all of the fears, frustrations and guilts my clients may be feeling. We cry together, we laugh together, and we work through all that has been holding us back. It's a meeting of minds that I simply cannot describe. Every connection is beautifully unique.

> *"Sustained change only happens when we shift at an emotional rather than logical level."*

— ROBIN SHARMA

The biggest and most sustained turning points in my life have come from making the investment in me. As a Mum that's something which in itself was such a battle. The investment of time, precious time, and also not forgetting financially too. We are so very often down at the bottom of our invisible hierarchical lists that we find it extremely difficult to justify investing in ourselves. When I invested in my first coach, I remember the mind whisperings having a good old natter about how better that money could have been spent and a few low blows of selfishness were mentioned on occasion too. But what I found was that investing in me at such a deep level was in actual fact encouraging me to grow in a way that supported my vision. My vision to be the 'yes Mummy', the Mummy that paves the way and provides for my family in more ways than one, a vision that means that I show my children a version of the world as it should be. Investing in me and expanding my support systems also meant that I could be the best version of myself whilst doing all of that. I had someone in my corner. Listening, holding space for me, and helping me to see the light in the deep moments of dark.

All of this paved the way for me to be talking to you here today. Realising my dream. Living my purpose. Shining my light and sharing my true voice.

And so I will leave you with a few final words:

You don't have to know the destination; you don't have to know the perfect how.

Just have the desire to start, to take imperfect action.

You owe it to yourself to discover your true calling and to share it with the world.

You owe it to yourself to grab your dreams with both hands and not watch from afar, not be a spectator to your perfect life.

You have a voice, a message: draw courage and clarity, and shine bright, beautiful you.

The dots only make sense when you can join them. But they always join in the end.

With Love and Light

Stacey xxx

ABOUT THE AUTHOR
STACEY KNIGHT-JONES

As a Clarity and Mindset Coach, Stacey specialises in supporting her clients to master their mindset and in understanding what their true life passions are. Whilst removing old habits she supports them to take consistent, aligned action in order to create a life that they love, their own 'Life by Design'.

After spending most of her career in the Education sector and spending over eight years in the higher Education sector alone, Stacey developed an interest in personal development and the psychology around our search for clarity and confidence and 'something more to life than this'.

Stacey started her first business in 2011 after having her son and quickly realised her passion for supporting others to become their own version of successful and to live a life that supports their desires as parents. This even now is at the very heart of everything she teaches. In 2019 she became certified in Neuro Linguistic Programming, Life Purpose and Breakthrough Coaching and now uses these methods to compliment the work that she does.

Stacey lives in Staffordshire, UK, with her husband and two children and can often be found walking in nature (coffee in hand) with the next episode of her favourite podcast in her ears or deep in the throes of mummy duties, with swimming, ballet and karate lessons galore.

Contact:

Website: www.staceyknight-jones.com
Email: stacey@knightjones.co.uk

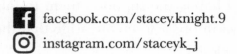 facebook.com/stacey.knight.9
instagram.com/staceyk_j

TABASSUM SABIR

I always thought I was not very confident. I can remember from a young age, one of my teachers expressing her concern to my Dad - she is extremely bright, but she never raises her hand. My Dad, as encouraging as always, would go home and have a chat with me. Don't be shy he would say. If you know something, raise your hand and make sure you participate.

It was only recently I discovered how my Dad has contributed significantly to my confidence throughout my life.He has always been an encourager, a cheerleader but it was always very subtle; he wasn't particularly explicit but at the same time I always felt it was there. He didn't have the opportunities we had.

Coming to the UK at a tender young age he started work as soon as possible to support his family. He got married to my Mum, and was soon enough supporting his own children and wife as well as his entire family back home (something he would never be appreciated for, let alone get his rights).

He never once let me or feel like I couldn't do anything. He still is a firm believer in education and opportunity, and regardless of the lack of confidence I always seem to have had in myself, my greatest encouragers have come from my own direct family. I truly appreciate how blessed I am to have that; I realise that's not a reality for everyone. My siblings and my parents have always been amazing. Looking back now, I can say I had an extremely happy childhood given the difficulties my parents went through. I never felt without and I always felt loved.

My Mum has been chronically ill since I remember from my very early years. She became unwell, when I was quite young, around the age of eight or nine is my first memory. It was then I began to realise how empathetic I am - even if it was subconsciously. I could feel an energy shift in a room, I had great sensory acuity, I noticed people's body language and their words. I now realise especially how I notice when people's words are incongruent with everything else.

I empathised with the stresses my Dad had to deal with balancing work, his children and the continuous trips to the hospitals whenever my Mum's condition worsened, which was A LOT. She finally got diagnosed with Ulcerative Colitis, an ulcerated and inflamed intestine which was irreversible, and it was going to affect her long term which ultimately meant it affected us all. Still, to keep her spirits up we always were by her side one by one, whoever was available that evening, and I am grateful to say that being of service to my parents has been my greatest honour to date.

My Dad encouraged me to go to University, something I wasn't too keen on, but he wanted me to have an education to fall back on. My confidence and self-esteem grew. I secured employment in one of the top pharmaceutical companies in the world and it was a stone's throw away from home. I felt truly blessed. Things couldn't have been better.

It was when I went out into the big world by myself, that my experiences began to shape my confidence and my self-worth (or lack thereof). You as the reader will notice I state MY lack of self-worth because ultimately this came down to me: whilst certain situations brought out other people's lack of my worth in their life it came down to my own lack of self-worth that ultimately broke me. I would love to fill you with a sob story of events and people who wronged me but actually whilst life happened (as it tends to) I felt myself spiralling out of control - life kept happening and my self-esteem was at an all-time low. No matter how much my close circle told me how amazing they thought I was - I didn't see it in myself. I blamed people close to me but deep down I knew there was something inside me.

I digress. When finally my life changed, I was not around the encouragement and consistent feeling of worthiness and my life changed very quickly. I had two children and looking back now I can almost certainly say during the turn of events around my firstborn's arrival I was a shell of myself. As a lot of first time Mums will relate, I had to give up work and become a stay at home mum (something I wanted to do more than anything in the world, to be with my baby); my life turned upside down as I gave up work but at the same time I was torn. I had lost my independence and my identity.

I had worked since the age of fifteen and for the first time I had to stay at home, and it wasn't my parents' home. I felt a bit lost. I all of a sudden found myself experiencing my first dose of lack of self-worth. Many ladies will relate to the constant criticism of having your first child and everything you do is just questioned and compared to so many others; it's not something just Muslim women will relate to. It's a little sad to admit but Facebook became my lifeline. I had not connected with a lot of mums locally as I was working so instead I connected with people online. I look back now and think I am so grateful - the many groups I joined with new mamas from all walks of life and they were experiencing the same hardships and difficulties, the constant criticism and comparisons. It is rife in our society and it is a disease. It was at a time when I was becoming frustrated constantly searching to prove myself in other ways as a woman, as an independent Muslim woman that I could have it all and I will. I was desperate to have an identity which was not related to my children and my husband - an identity of my own. For so long I had been a research scientist: now what would I be? Who would I be?

I have entrepreneurial blood, I am sure of it - having several businesses from the age of 22 I was passionate to have a side income and run a business from home around my kids one day. I was spiritually connected, and my faith has always led me so I was sure it would lead me where I needed to be now. It was at this time I was running an online modest clothing boutique and I had also qualified as a Makeup Artist just before leaving work for maternity and trying to fit that work in on the weekends when someone could look after the baby (no easy feat when breast-feeding!).

Out of the blue one day, when things were really frustrating me, all of a sudden, I connected with someone on Facebook about a Network Marketing Opportunity. I procrastinated for two weeks before signing up and before I knew it, I was earning an income from home around my now two gorgeous boys. I was living the dream; I was working from home around my babies and had my own income in a business I was super passionate about. But no matter how much I was praised for my hard work and success I lacked seeing it myself. It was through Network Marketing I discovered personal development work. Since then my life has never been the same.

My business went through ups and downs as I battled with my own ego consistently. My confidence grew as I started to build a team and present live videos on my social media accounts - something I was terrified to do for months. All of a sudden, this newfound confidence began to grow; it felt familiar. But this was different. I had to encourage myself and it was draining. My father was no longer constantly around me and my mother's health was quite bad this year meaning he was very occupied with her health - I felt bad for constantly needing him to tell me I could do it (even though both Mum and Dad did anyway!).

They say events are really powerful in Network Marketing companies and I can see why. Seeing all the success stories and what people had battled with, really started to resonate with me and I began to emotionally connect to my goals. When I first started, I didn't even know what my goals were. It had been so long since I had thought about what I wanted. I felt almost selfish for wanting anything for myself at all. It was through this journey I found that I had let so many events from my past shape my present and if I didn't do something about it now, I was going to ruin my future. I couldn't allow that. I had to be amazing for my boys.

I came across a business coach who I started to work with. She was amazing too - I suddenly began to notice how I was beginning to connect with some amazing women who had been through awfully traumatic experiences and still succeeded - this strengthened my belief that I could do this, I just had this constant ongoing battle with myself, this little voice in my head telling me I couldn't do it. It was exhausting.

Something had to change: my mindset needed work and my lack of consistency was giving me bursts of energy and then nothing at all. I would self-sabotage in ways that were not obvious to me at that time then but are crystal clear to me now. Why is that? Because all these amazing women that had got through it had one thing in common - personal development and coaching.

I watched a close friend of mine completely transform with coaching. I was in awe - she had been through so much. How did this happen? My business coach had qualified with some new skills and was now offering emotional mastery coaching. With some extremely surprising turn of events, some intense coaching sessions and lots of tears and frustration along the way, I finally figured out what I needed to get my lack of self-worth and lack of self-esteem back. With an amazing circle of supporters combined I finally managed to break free from holding myself back. It's so easy to become ungrateful when you feel like life is happening to you and not for you.

I decided to relaunch my businesses and train in coaching too, using a number of therapies that helped me. These women changed my life and if I have the opportunity to impact just one woman's life with my message then I will feel like I have contributed to saving one person going through a similar downward spiral of lack of self-worth and lack of self-esteem to myself. It will literally mean the world to me. But that's not my goal; it's much bigger.

There's a saying that goes 'women are half of society and they raise the other half of society.' It's so important to have strong, resilient women who do not constantly beat themselves up for being human. For feeling things, for experiencing things, however it is when those emotions take over and you can no longer see the light at the end of the tunnel. Being on a constant emotional roller coaster is draining, and until I was able to work on myself and actually find Coaching and Time Line Therapy with my constant belief in Allah to change everything for me, I really do believe I still would have been on that emotional roller coaster today.

I am a firm believer that Allah (you may call it the universe, God, source) sends people to you at the right time and I believe every page in my story has been written by the greatest author. If I had not had those experiences, I would not be the person I am today. Do I regret them? Not for a second. It led me to this place and it's a place I am truly grateful for every day. I realised that Allah kept me very protected and averse to things for a long time and only showed me things when I was ready to deal with them. When these amazing coaches and powerful women were present in my life. When I was ready to make a change, not only for my own future but for women everywhere.

I now have a one to one coaching programme and an online membership programme, both of which I love. I am so excited to be helping women and it absolutely makes me jump out of bed every morning to serve the ladies I connect with. A content mother, wife, daughter, sister really does make for a happy home. It also helps us from passing down traumas generation after generation. The buck stops with me.

You see, the above story doesn't sound too bad, does it? No major trauma, no huge losses. That's because I missed out all of that as I got used to telling my story by blocking out the really bad stuff! I suffered from kidney failure at the age of twelve. I am grateful to say that I survived that time and recovered by having dialysis. I remember that was the first time I had seen my really emotionally strong Dad cry. The doctors initially thought I had what Mum had and he was terrified as to what was to come like hospital stays and surgeries. I built a very close relationship with my Dad at this time: he was my first love, my Superhero.

Immediately after this experience, I also experienced sexual abuse. I was too scared to say anything to anyone for a long time until my best friend from school at the time found out I was seriously becoming careless and distracted. I started to skip school. She encouraged me to tell my family. That one experience shaped a lot of things in my life. But I did what I knew to do best. I suppressed it. I didn't have the tools to deal with it so I just put it in a box and in a place where I wouldn't need to deal with it.

How did this come out? In self-sabotaging behaviour. I went from being a good girl to being a rebel. I did many things I am not proud of, but I wouldn't change them because they shaped my journey to the person I am today. I found my solitude in faith. I started to pray a lot and finally I felt like I had a connection I would never lose. Until I did, and then the self-sabotage would come back, in very unhealthy ways. Anything I had good I would try to sabotage, unknowingly at this point. I couldn't sit in my good feelings for very long at all, that wasn't normal for me. I lived in a bubble expecting everyone to be as loving and as supportive as my own family and quickly realised this was not the case at all. It was like the carpet had been pulled from under my feet. Add that to getting married and starting a whole new life, in a whole new place and then having babies pretty quickly because I didn't want to feel left behind. I wanted to be doing what everyone else was doing. Getting married, having kids, buying a house, buying a new car, two amazing holidays a year... the list was endless about the life I had expected but I did nothing to actually to secure that life.

When I couldn't even face praying anymore, I don't think I held enough self-worth or self-esteem to even believe I was deserving of that connection. I was at my lowest low and yet I didn't know how I got there. The sad thing is many faithful people get there. I now felt more alone then I had ever, and I was surrounded by people. That was part of my escape - keep distracted and then you won't have to deal with it. I was on a downward spiral of self-sabotage surrounded by constant negativity and nothing could give me energy. I was taking loads of supplements; I tried all the health and wellness products I could get my hands on and changed my diet several times. Everything I had tried in the past wasn't working any more. I felt like I was depressed and didn't want a diagnosis because that would mean my kids getting taken away from me (this is what would happen in my head).

So, then I did what any woman does, go to YouTube, self-development books, Podcasts, you name it I had it. I spent the most time on Facebook and started to follow more inspiring people, getting frustrated why I couldn't get to the bottom of MY issues. I couldn't do anything and for someone who had always been so determined, who always did what she said, it was disabling. I couldn't even look in the mirror, I didn't recognise the woman looking back at me. I always used to catch my coach on live videos (one of the best marketing tools ever). I had been watching her for a while and as she started to share her story I realised how it resonated with my own. *I had been suppressing my emotions all this time. Really?* I would always cry or get angry. They were my two go to emotions! I never experienced feeling them to this level before in my life. Something was starting to make sense.

What if it didn't work? Where would I go? What would I do next? The best part of coaching is the pre-frame! You are either ALL IN or ALL OUT. Even when I reached out to her for coaching, I sabotaged that too. I got scared. It was money I didn't have. I booked in with her in January and didn't return the coaching agreement. When the problem was too much of a problem, I went back to her in March and her costs had gone up, but I no longer cared. I had seen a friend's transformation with her. The feedback she was getting was phenomenal. I knew this journey was going to be tough and it was a long road ahead (twelve weeks of coaching when you want instant results is A LOT to ask of an impatient person). But life was no longer worth living the way it was right now. It was ALL or nothing, I was ALL IN.

I hadn't processed my emotions. As coaching began that became more apparent. I had misunderstood religious texts to understand it was ok for me to be oppressed rather than stand up to it, a mistake many Muslim women make. Not to take a stand or to create arguments with anyone but to understand our own self-worth, our inner power, our value. Allah (or the universe if that's what you prefer) created you for a reason! There is no one like you and I just think that reminder in itself is amazing.

Some people start the coaching process and think it will split relationships, but it doesn't. It empowers you to make choices that fit with your values. If there are unprocessed negative emotions "active" in your body the subconscious mind will eventually over time remind you of those things. It's a means of self-protection as we develop from old brain to new brain mentality. Our reptilian brain is always looking to save us and sometimes that's not in healthy ways. By suppressing emotions, if that makes you cry and feel rubbish and not want to eat or eat a lot, it will protect you from that by saying, 'ok let's not process it, let's just forget about it.' But the pattern emerges when a familiar situation or emotion comes up again and again. The more your emotional cup fills up the less space it has to absorb an emotion - then you become short and snappy. You know when you have had one of those days when everything starts really bad and all day things go bad? You are so annoyed and wound up and then someone cuts you up on the motorway. When you get home your parcel has not been posted because it needs a signature and then the kids are being super noisy today so that you just snapped? Anyone relate? It's because you have been dealing with "stuff" all day, that's why you snap. Your cup became so full that you no longer have any more space for "stuff" and now it needs to be released. Quickly as possible before you know it you have yelled at the kids and they are in tears. You feel like rubbish but then momentarily release has given you some relief. But now you feel guilt.

This is how our emotional cup fills up from the day we are born! If we do not process those emotions, they keep showing up. This is the part I find so fascinating and although I was extremely skeptical to begin with, I honestly believed this was perhaps something that fell outside the realms of my faith (although again that was a belief I developed) I realised that couldn't be further then the truth.

When I am working with clients on a one to one basis, the best way I find is to start with the end in mind. No, that's not supposed to be depressing, I do not mean the end of your life per se. I do mean think about what you want in your life. What you want to have achieved, what can make the impact and what can you do to get there.

Often my clients will say, 'I am not sure about impact.' Well no matter what you do, you will impact at least one other person in your life. So, if it's easier to digest, think about impacting just one person in your life and the ripple effect that will have. Just one. Even if that is your child, a family member, a neighbour, a friend. See, so many people don't achieve the goals because they call them dreams, and that's where they end up staying.

It's really funny how life will bring you full circle too! When I had completed a GNVQ in Health and Social Care at college, I was made fun of by a lot of people. The thing is I wanted to get into social work, and this was a good starting point for me. I also did A/S level Psychology, so I kind of feel I was destined on this path of helping people all my life. I just didn't know how. I knew I wouldn't have the emotional resilience needed for social work and there was too much red tape to follow, for good reason I am sure. I was fascinated with the human mind and psyche. I think deep down I wanted to be a coach even then, I just didn't know it existed. I am always known for helping people, sometimes at my own detriment but usually it was a selfless kind of help. I now know this is one of the values that is extremely important to me.

So, I ended up doing a science degree. I don't regret that either, I really had to prove my own resilience to myself. I actually thought I would fail until my brother Fahim (another serial supporter) told me failure wasn't an option for me. I still remember that phone conversation like it was yesterday. I never looked back. I completed my degree with Mum being constantly in and out of hospital and it was really hard work. I would have to re-sit exams because of missing them with Mum being sick. It was a tough time but through it all I always felt supported by my siblings and my parents. I digress.

Always listen to your gut. I knew deep down I wanted to help people, and the only time I felt out of alignment was when I focused on chasing money (making sales) rather than providing an amazing service. Whenever I felt out of alignment my body told me through my gut. This whole time I had related that all back to my mum's health, but it was actually where I held a lot of my trauma.

Only when I actually processed the root of the trauma (my emotions) was I able to do things I couldn't imagine saying about myself three years ago. I would write my own book, which is making me smile as I write this. I want to own a business I can run online. I want to work with women. I want to help them master their emotions. I want to have a fragrance franchise. I want to feature in the media. I want to be on TV. I want to be someone other women come to for help. I want to be a leader in my niche. I want to help women set up an online business they are passionate about. I want to show women how to make money using social media without being spammy.

What if I told you all of the above is everything I have achieved so far? Do I have more goals? Yes, absolutely. These are my steppingstones to my ultimate goal. I am clear on it. I can see it, taste it, hear it, feel it. I can literally see it as a movie plays in my mind through visualisation, another skill learnt that makes the coaching process more powerful. But did you know there are questions that you can actually ask yourself to get a well-formed outcome? Stuff that will actually ensure your goal is powerful and congruent and you won't sabotage it at any given point. You can get the well-formed questions on my website tabassumsabir.com.

So now I had all the skills in place, I started to become a student! I became obsessed with my goal (anyone who knows me, knows I do not do things in halves). The mindset was finally in the right place and the sabotaging blocks removed. The great thing is whenever something comes up for me, I just go back to my coach. I tried to do that by myself for a while but that wasn't working; it really slowed down my progress and I had things to do, people to impact.

When my mind actually opened up to all the possibilities at my fingertips (no pun intended) I then found everything just clicked into place like a jigsaw puzzle. The pieces all fit together so beautifully. Everything that led up to that point (even all my steppingstone businesses) had led me to a point where I could finally help others. All around my children, I had an identity other than being a Mum, and that was really important to me, but when the kids were home, they had their Mum. There wasn't going to be any Mum guilt and I had realised no one was going to help me with childcare, so I had to create a business for me, that worked on my terms. Something I didn't believe could ever exist.

You see, I used to think my sensitive, kind, calm, loving nature was always holding me back. You had to be cutthroat in the business world to be successful, right? Super wrong! Since being in this world I connected with the most amazing women who actually experience joy in helping other people succeed. So now I seek out women from home running an online business, someone with skills who can help me achieve my goals and I help them achieve theirs. It's a world I never knew existed and I am so grateful every day to be a part of it.

The amazing thing about coaching, I discovered, is how it can completely turn your life around, just from changing the way you think. Coaching breaks all the barriers of culture and yet maintains your dignity because you show up as your best self. You are not bitter, you are kind; you are not sad, you are content; you are no longer fearful. I feel so truly blessed to be Muslim because without my faith and the fact I could sit on my prayer mat and cry my heart out when I needed to, I do not believe I would have got through what I did.

I encourage you all, if you are finding yourself on an emotional roller coaster, just for a minute be true to yourself and ask yourself why you are not allowing yourself to get off the ride. Ask yourself what it will take to be free of this. You do not have to go through so much pain, which is stopping you from being your true self, your higher self. The journey of working on yourself is not an easy one but the outcome is the most beautiful thing ever and that's why it's become my lifelong passion to help other women break through.

Confidence. Some girls have it, some girls don't. At least that's what I thought.

I would like to take this opportunity to express my infinite gratitude to my family, especially my parents. Without them, I would not have the grit and resilience I have today.

To my siblings, my loved ones, my closest friends (you know who you are) and to those who listened to me for hours on end, especially my wonderful coach, my gratitude here will never be enough, I appreciate you.

To my husband, my children, the reason I wore courage as my crown, thank you for always supporting me and giving me a reason to be more than I ever thought I could be, constantly believing in me and encouraging me.

To those who came into my life to teach me the most valuable of lessons, thank you. I am grateful as you helped me to grow: the negatives and the positives all taught me something...and I will never stop growing.

Tabassum Sabir is a soul centered heart led Self Mastery, Self Esteem and Success Coach to women in business, mums and passionate ladies everywhere. She is owner at Be-you-tiful coaching and mentoring, an expert in her field as Emotional Mastery Coach, a certified NLP (neuro-linguistic programming) Master Practitioner, a Master Coach, a Master Practitioner in TimeLine Therapy and a Master Hypnotherapist.

Having appeared on Takbeer TV and British Muslim TV, positioned as an emotional mastery and self-esteem expert, she is passionate in sharing her life experiences to help ensure other women not just survive but blossom in all areas of their lives.

She is also due to soon be launching her joint venture podcast called Mindset Matters which addresses current issues that women experience.

Her mission is to help women flourish into their best self, using the tools and skills she has learned and developed.

She believes that women are here to serve their higher purpose in life as emotional leaders and be fully aligned in what they do so they can be leaders in their own right, whether that be in business or in their personal life, to succeed and Be-you-tiful.

Contact: Website: www.tabassumsabir.com

facebook.com/tabassum.sabir

twitter.com/tabassumsabir

instagram.com/tabassumsabir

linkedin.com/in/tabassumsabir

pinterest.com/tabassumssabir

TARA CORBETT

I went through my whole life thinking that there was absolutely no way that I would ever have a good body. I remember clear as day believing this to be wholeheartedly true. Even just writing that down now seems almost laughable at how far removed I was then. I had a very clear and set notion of who I was and what my body was capable of. And what it definitely was not capable of, was being thin.

I was never the small girl growing up. I was always quite tall, being one of the tallest ones in the class and standing at the back for all the school pictures (luckily, when puberty finally hit the boys, they caught up). But as well as being tall, I was also bigger. I was never cute and dainty like my friends. I would look at their little legs, with their pointed-out knees, and stick thin arms, and compare them to my own. Solid. I was certainly not overweight as a child, but I had a bigger build and certainly a little chub. And I was extremely aware of it.

When I try to think back on it now, I can't recall a time when I wasn't aware of what I ate. I learnt from my surroundings, and my mother and grandmother were certainly active in the whole crash diet and yo-yo culture, going up and down marginally in weight. They each had had their own experiences of going on many diets and restricting their food intake. I would watch them talk about their bodies and talk about their desire to change them. I learnt what 'good' food consisted of (it was the 90s, and so we're talking a lot of low fat yoghurt, fat free salad dressings, and rice cakes here!). And I learnt what 'bad' food was; and that if I didn't want to be fat, I should be avoiding eating those foods.

Except I was only a kid, and with that came the inability to restrict and diet in the way an adult can. I couldn't just *not* have all the cheese and crisps at family gatherings and birthday parties, with it all spread out in front of me. Especially when I would see other children, with their enviable skinny arms and legs, indulging in all the snacks. And so I would just eat it anyway. And then I would feel terrible about it. I would wonder why I was cursed with the inability to resist the food, and wonder why I couldn't just eat what I wanted and be small. Needless to say, the food guilt started early, and it was very strong from the start.

Because I always had an understanding of what food would make me fat versus what wouldn't (my child logic and terminology in full swing here), I didn't like to eat the 'bad' foods in public. I had already formed the logic and belief that eating those items was embarrassing. I didn't want to seem like it was my fault that I was bigger, and I associated eating those 'bad' foods as being shameful. And so I would always play down the amount I ate around friends, at school, or at other friends' homes.

But I certainly ate it all in private.

I remember I would come home from school, and just absolutely let loose in the kitchen. The first thing I would do as soon as I was home would be to bee line to the kitchen. I would then stand and hover in the fridge, eating anything I could find that would make me feel good and comforted in that moment. I was a big fan of leftovers and cheese and crackers (not much has really changed on that front!). I would always eat it standing up, as in my opinion that felt as though it wasn't *real* if I was standing. The second I had to put it on a plate and sit down, it suddenly became a conscious choice to eat. But if I was stood up, I could just enter the trance and pretend like it had never happened.

Except then I would have the hard evidence that I was eating too much when I would look at myself. I was starting to teeter on being a bit bigger than I felt comfortable being. I was starting to really zero in on different aspects of my body, and critiquing myself. I felt like my weight was holding me back, and I didn't like how it made me feel when I would see myself. And so by the time I was thirteen, I made the conscious decision to do something about it.

I then embarked on my very first diet when I was thirteen. Looking back now, I can't believe I was that concerned about my weight at that age. At the time, I was already concerned that my value as a person was being detracted from because of my body. I believed I was fat, and I hated it. I thought people were going to like me less because of my size. I was comparing myself to my friends and their bodies, and there was no doubt that I was the biggest one out of us all. I saw the other girls and how they looked, and I wanted to look on par when it came to my weight. I was starting to get attention from boys, but in my head I knew I could look so much better if I just lost some weight. I fully admit that even at such a young age, I generally thought my life would magically improve in all areas if I were to lose weight. This was the missing piece I needed to have everything click into place, and for me to really flourish in my teen years!

I told my mum my desire to go on a diet and lose weight, and she gave me Oprah's book on how she lost weight. (Make the Connection - 10 Steps to a Better Body and a Better Life, circa the 1990s. I've just looked it up, and you can still get it today on eBay for £2.25 - an absolute bargain!)

"Read this and follow her instructions to make sure you are doing it the healthy way," she told me. "And make sure you exercise!"

I soaked it all in. I read it with an intense sense of urgency. If this was how Oprah lost her hundreds of pounds, then I was going to follow her advice to a T. I mean, it was Oprah! She was such an inspiration, and so if she had advice on the topic, I was sure going to listen. I was going to adopt each and every rule, and then watch the transformation unfold before me.

And that was the start to my life with rules and restrictions around food. That was the start to my history of diets and needing to follow them to 100% perfection.

That being said, it really did work. I lost weight, and I loved being smaller. I felt like suddenly I was more myself, and I had the identity that I always knew I could be if my external appearance matched my expectations. I stuck to her rules for probably about a year and a half. I grew accustomed to avoiding 'bad' foods, and only eating small portions of 'good' food. I woke up and exercised every weekday morning, extra early to make sure I could get my metabolism fired up and going, just as Oprah suggested I do. I also went vegetarian at the time, largely due to the fact that I felt like I could avoid 'bad' foods a lot easier if I didn't eat meat (and half because my brother bet me that I couldn't do it. Classic little sister stubbornness!). Suddenly it became a lot easier to always order the salads at restaurants if you have to avoid all the meat options. The more rules I was adding and restricting myself with, the more success I was having. I couldn't have been happier that I had finally 'hacked' the way to lose weight and keep it off. I was beyond pleased with myself that I had gotten over my chubby past, and I could be this thinner version of myself. But all that being said, I was blissfully unaware of what was coming.

Because ultimately, I couldn't control my environment to follow Oprah's ten rules forever. There was no big moment in which I broke and fell off the wagon, but rather lots of small little moments that pushed me back to my old habits. Any time I experienced a bad emotion, I would start to turn back to my old friend to get me through - the fridge. Whenever I felt bad about myself, I soothed it with chocolate, cheese, and cookies. I was still maintaining my healthy exterior of selecting salads over sandwiches, and sushi over McDonalds; but I was cracking when it came to emotional eating.

This carried on throughout my teen years, into university, and then throughout my 20s. I had such a keen interest in nutrition, diets and exercise because I had such a personal investment in the topic. I was constantly aware of what I would eat, which worked both for me and against me. I would be beaming with pride when I chose to eat from the salad or sandwich bar at my dorm dining hall in uni. Or I would be telling myself I was dumb and fat for having cheesy fries and pasta one night. Every decision I made about food turned into a moral reflection of who I was, and I was so deep into this logic that I didn't even realise it was flawed. I thought it was just how I personally had to be in order to look good.

I learned a lot about nutrition at this time, which ultimately I am so grateful for as that really sparked the groundwork for becoming a nutritionist years later. I learnt what macronutrients were, and how I should be portioning my food intake. I learnt how to read a nutrition label, and what to look out for with ingredient lists on packages. I started learning average portion sizes, and started memorising how many calories were in certain foods.

I also got into the gym and properly working out. I had been a runner since I was thirteen, but learning what to do at the gym was certainly uncharted terrain for me. But I just put my head down and researched it all. I learned which exercises I should be doing for different areas of my body, and how to use all the different machines at the gym. I learnt what a proper squat and lunge were, and how to rotate my muscle groups throughout the week to customise a plan for myself.

As brilliant as it was to dive so deep into all this subject matter, I was doing it for the wrong reasons. I was doing it from a place of dislike for myself and my body. I wanted to lose weight and get thin, and I thought the only way to do that was to monitor everything I ate, try my best to avoid all the 'bad' foods, and work off all the calories I ate by going to the gym. I was very much into the logic that if I ate bad foods, I had to compensate by working out harder and longer. "You ate a shawarma after the bar last night, Tara: you'd better stay on that treadmill for sixty mins today."

Ironically, I was not in great shape through these years of obsession. Because as hard as I would try to diet perfectly, I never could. I would break the minute it was inconvenient. Or by the time the weekend came, I was ready to quit the diet and have all the drinks and all the junk food. I was very much in the party lifestyle during the weekend, and it conflicted massively with my healthy habits during the week.

I was putting far too much energy into dieting to perfection and I would need to then reward myself on Friday. I would of course then overdo it after a couple of glasses of wine, and eat all the snacks. I would then have a conversation in my head, rationalising why I could then eat everything and anything for the rest of the weekend, since I had already 'undone' all my hard work. "May as well make it really worth it then," I'd tell myself as I was buying £20 worth of cheese and chocolate at the Sainsburys Local across from my flat. Quickly followed, of course, with an, "It's fine though, because I will just be so strict come Monday, and go to the gym every morning before work next week."

The diet was always going to start back up on Monday. It was always going to be Monday that I got SERIOUS about it this time, and would lose all the weight and transform into this perfect, banging 10/10 version of myself. It was always starting Monday. On Monday it was going to be different this time.

I was always visualising my life suddenly becoming perfect once I lost weight. I had a very clear visual of my most ideal self, and I knew I could be her once I lost weight. I would suddenly have the most amazing wardrobe, long perfect hair, flawless makeup, and heels always on point. I would have a smoking hot boyfriend who was absolutely obsessed with me, and commitment wouldn't even be an issue. And I would have an epic social life, out all the time and just living large.

But it always started with first losing the weight and getting thin. I tied my value and self-worth so deeply into my size and body, and I truly thought it was one of the most important things about me. I thought that the thinner I was, the more people would like me, and the more attention I would get. And with that came the thought that every time something negative happened in my life, it was because of my size.

Any time I didn't get the guy I was interested in, I thought it was because I was fat. When one of my long-term boyfriends cheated on me with a girl he worked with, I remember just instantly comparing her body to mine. Was she thinner than me? Could I have avoided this if I'd just actually lost that ten pounds I'd been meaning to? Did he cheat because he thinks I've let myself go and I'm now too fat for him?

One of the most defining moments that started my transformation with food and my body was when I found out I was pregnant. For the first time in my entire life, my focus on my body was not on losing weight. It was not on critiquing all the areas that were too big, jiggly, and ugly. I suddenly didn't need to check my stomach every morning to see if it looked flat or bloated.

I had to just let go of the notion of controlling what I ate and let my body do its thing. If it was going to start gaining weight, I had to just sit back and let it happen. And it was fucking liberating.

For the first time, I could sit down and eat a full plate of pasta with garlic bread on the side and feel nothing. I wouldn't feel guilty, shameful, or that I would need to compensate by working out extra hard the next day. I could have a full plate of biscuits for lunch and feel happy about that decision (yes, totally happened one day. The nutritionist had nine biscuits in the middle of the day, and then napped right after). Food suddenly lost all its meaning to me, and was nothing but a source of physical need, and a bit of happiness and enjoyment through those nine months.

Exercise suddenly became important for my health, and not just important as a means to burn calories. I was going on long walks because it felt nice and I could clear my head, not because I was a slave to hitting my 10k steps a day. I started doing yoga because it helped my lower back pain in my third trimester and loved it. I had always avoided yoga before, because I thought it was too slow and didn't burn enough calories to really 'count' as working out.

Although I would never claim I enjoyed pregnancy, letting my body grow the way it wanted to was the biggest wakeup call I could have ever had. I ended up gaining more than thirty kilos throughout the nine months. Although stepping on the scale the day before I gave birth to see 101 KG was certainly shocking, I delivered the most perfect 8lb 5oz healthy baby girl, and in that moment I did not care one bit.

But that also meant I had the biggest weight loss journey of my life ahead of myself. I had all the knowledge to do it with my background and qualifications, but my ability to do it had to change. I was now busier than ever, and frankly had no time to BS myself with all my stories about how to lose weight. I knew what I had to do, and I just needed to get it done without the obsession around food. Without the hours of time at the gym. And without turning to food the moment I felt stressed and over-whelmed in my new demanding role of mummy.

Interestingly enough, the beginning of my postpartum weight loss journey coincided with the beginning of my journey into manifestation and the laws of the universe. Up until I became a mother, I had an extremely narrow view of the world. My experience in the world was black and white, and I deemed anyone spiritual as having lost the plot a bit. I had never meditated, and the last thing I was ever going to do was sit there and chant affirmations to myself. That just wasn't me, and my mind was very closed off to it. I can remember so vividly listening to a podcast that I was such an avid fan of, and Gabby Bern-stein was a guest on one episode. Only ten minutes in, and I was turning it off thinking, "Oh my god, who *is* this woman? Ugh, pass." Which now makes me laugh to myself, because I admire her so much! I just wasn't ready for her at that time (the universe was having me wait!).

But I knew I was going to go all in on my business, and I was going to make my success inevitable as a nutritionist. And quite honestly, I didn't want to waste any time working at a less than fulfilling job now as a mum, so I was going to grind. And with that grind came a whole lot of research into how successful people achieved their successes. I'm definitely a firm believer that success leaves clues, so I dove headfirst into all the content and information I could find about how to build a brand and a business. And the recurring theme I kept hearing explained over and over again was mindset. And mindset quickly trickled down into the law of attraction and manifestation.

I started where most people start - The Secret. I soaked it all in, and that just opened my mind and led me to believe there was so much more to learn. I had literally just hit the tip of the iceberg. I was starting to believe in the power of the mind, and the power in how I could decide the thoughts in my head.

Up until that point, I did not even believe that I could control the words in my head. It was as if they had a mind of their own, and I was this innocent bystander just shrugging her shoulders thinking, "Well, I can't help it." But I was waking up and realising I could most definitely help it. I could change my thoughts, and thus change my life.

And this realisation was suddenly extremely relevant to my postpartum weight loss journey.

What if I was blocking the release of weight through constantly hating my body?

What if all the obsession around what to eat and fearing being 'fat' was attracting the fat to me?

And what if all the self-limiting beliefs I had in regard to my identity with food and my weight were not true, but actually extremely false? I always believed that in order for me to be thin and in shape, I had to work extremely hard. It was unnatural for me to be small. I believed that I was born to be a bit thicker, and I had my crappy metabolism to blame for that. And losing weight was difficult and torturous, but it had to be done, otherwise I'd look like I've let myself go.

I was having my light bulb moment. I had spent my whole life looking at food and losing weight as a surface level problem. And it was anything but. I finally figured out that I could never achieve the results and transformation I was after because I wasn't doing the internal work. Actually, everything I was thinking and feeling internally was in direct conflict with losing weight. I was fighting an uphill battle and I wasn't even aware of it. I thought I was doing everything right, and whatever was missing was simply out of my control.

As clichéd as it sounds, I realised you really do need to love yourself from the inside before you are ever happy with what you see on the outside. People say this statement for a reason - and that reason was no longer one I would roll my eyes at. And I'm not talking about looking at yourself and your size 16 body and convincing yourself that you are a Victoria's Secret model. And I'm not talking about suddenly posting pictures of yourself in your lingerie with a few rolls on your stomach on Instagram with #lovey-ourself.

I'm referring to just being so in love with your life and yourself, that weight loss isn't your main goal any more. Weight loss and being thin will no longer be the ultimate sign of validation and acceptance from others. That being this super thin and lean version of yourself won't make your life perfect. And magical things don't happen when you suddenly fit into a size 6 dress.

Having this penny drop was the best thing that could have happened to my mind and perception of my body. Because I was able to mend my beliefs around what it took to lose weight, I stopped dieting to extremes. I wasn't tracking everything I ate and obsessing about if it was on plan or not. I suddenly had no expectations about a time frame for losing the weight; it was no longer a case of "I'd better get this over in six weeks so then I can actually LIVE again." I was finally able to use all the positive knowledge I knew about nutrition and apply it properly, from a completely different state.

It was work, but I did it. I completely rewrote my story and identity around food and my body. Thoughts and beliefs around diet culture that I had ingrained in my mind since I was thirteen have been erased, and I've been able to raise my frequency so damn high that I finally don't even think about my body most days. I choose healthy foods, I exercise, and I'm the healthiest and leanest I have ever been (and that's post baby). I show up every day as the person I always secretly knew I could be, but I could never figure out to materialise her. Figuring out how to put all these parts into play and action them to achieve an unbelievable transformation has put my life on a completely different trajectory than one I ever thought was possible. I've found a purpose in helping as many mums as possible do exactly the same thing, and transform themselves into the happiest, most confident version of themselves. I feel as though I have a purpose now, and it has nothing to do with myself and my worth. But rather it has everything to do with helping other mums feel as liberated and amazing as I feel. Because when you have a fulfilled and unstoppable mum at the head of the household, it trickles down to the kids and family at large. A new cycle of empowered children is released into the world, and that in itself makes me so damn excited.

If I could give any woman who resonates with my story advice, it really would be to invest the time and energy to get off the damn diet cycle. So if you are:

- Still trying to find that magical diet that will suddenly 'hack' your weight problems and transform your body overnight
- Still going on and off the same extreme, carb-less diets hoping it will work this time, on the 88th attempt
- Doing everything you can to follow the diet to 100% perfection, only to crash and burn at the first hurdle because it gets to be too hard
- Thinking that this time will be different, only to

never try anything different in terms of your approach

Because ending the emotional diet drama really doesn't have to mean 'letting yourself go'. When you stop dieting to extremes, you're not suddenly admitting defeat and that you are destined to be overweight for the rest of your life. It actually means the opposite - it means you will get to the size you would previously only dream about.

It's about so much more than just the foods you are putting into your mouth, but rather the words you're putting into your mind. It's about the transition of getting to the place where you:

- Stop stressing about food and what you should or shouldn't be eating
- Stop staring at other women and wonder why you're not as thin as them or don't look as great
- Lose the annoying weight that's keeping you from being who you truly want to be
- Wear the clothes you want to, and confidently know you look amazing without worrying about how your body looks
- End all the shame and guilt associated with eating those 'bad' foods

Because all of this is extremely possible and completely achievable once you make the decision to do something different. Once you decide to work on the internal shifts needed to enable weight loss and freedom from the obsession with food.

It's completely achievable for you, and within your reach. It's about making the decision to try something different and have the most liberating glow up possible.

ABOUT THE AUTHOR
TARA CORBETT

Tara Corbett is a certified nutritionist and qualified health and wellness coach. She works exclusively with women who are looking to end the constant diet cycling, lose weight, and quit the obsessions with their body and food.

Tara quickly discovered through her work as a nutritionist that the missing piece in so many weight loss journeys was the mindset and thought-work involved, which is why she has developed a much more holistic approach in her programmes. She combines elements of NLP, nutritional science, strategic habit building, and identity work in order to transform women's bodies and minds.

Her mission is to liberate women from the horrible diet culture and to transform their relationship with food and their bodies. She believes that women can accomplish so much more as mothers, partners, and in business/at work when they uplevel their confidence in this way. It trickles down to all other aspects of their life, and it's something she wants to see embedded in everyone she comes into contact with.

Contact

Email: hi@taracorbett.co.uk
Website: www.taracorbett.co.uk

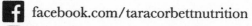 facebook.com/taracorbettnutrition
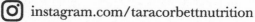 instagram.com/taracorbettnutrition